Byron Trowbridge   January 19, 1981

By The Editors Of Consumer Guide®

MODEL MILITARY

Beekman House

New York

Contents

Copyright© 1979 Publications International, Ltd.
All rights reserved.
Printed in the United States of America

This edition published by:
Beekman House
A Division of Crown Publishers, Inc.
One Park Avenue
New York, N.Y. 10016

Library of Congress Catalog Card Number: 79-64869
ISBN: 0-517-294613

Photo Credits: cover — ESCI, Mike Haggar, MRC-Tamiya, Revell, U.S. Airfix; photographic assistance — The Hobby Chest, Skokie, Illinois, and The Squadron Shop, Elmhurst, Illinois; photography — Doug Mitchel

Introduction

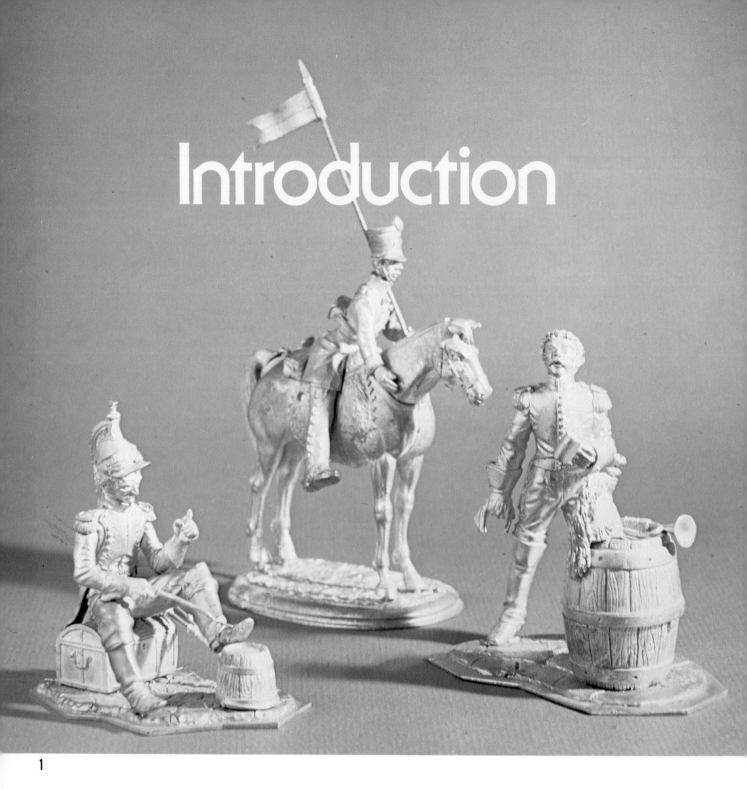

1

IN SOME DARK, primeval forest many thousands of years ago, a few cavemen banded together and attacked another caveman to take his food from him. Even through the dimness of his primitive mind, the caveman whose food had been taken knew that he could not fight the others alone to take back what was rightfully his. So he joined some neighboring cave dwellers in pursuit of those who had attacked him. This was probably the way organized warfare began.

Ever since that time, the history of mankind has been one long conflict, interrupted only occasionally by brief interludes of peace. Warfare has been a part of man's existence from the days when Alexander the Great set out to expand his empire; the tradition continued when Hannibal led his elephants across the Alps, as the barbarians of the Dark Ages sacked the civilized world, as the crusaders marched against the Muslims, as Frederick the Great of Prussia came to power, as the Union Blues and Confederate Grays took up arms. In this century, wars have been fought in the snows of Russia,

2

3

the jungles of Vietnam and the deserts of the Middle East.

Long after the end of each war, the winners and the losers alike have continued to talk of the valor of their comrades; the evil of their enemies.

Though war can tear apart families, countries, whole cultures, the selflessness and bravery that spring to life with a call to duty for a just cause is something that can unite a people. And even the most hateful of would-be conquerors can somehow be admired for their strategic skills.

Conflict is what provides the basic plot for nearly all poetry, novels, drama, operas. The stories of men and women in combat have been depicted in these art forms, as well as in painting and music. They conjure up memories that are at once saddening and thrilling, thoughts of suffering and poignant moments of camaraderie, visions of colorful ceremony and devastated battlefields.

Another art form has evolved throughout the history of warfare — that of military modeling. In this art, craft and hobby (it really must be thought of as

5

4

all three), people of all ages and of all different levels of skill can re-create events of the past. The result is pleasure in the construction and finishing of the model, as well as pride in its display.

The hobby of military modeling is truly a broad one. It offers something to the person who likes to work with his hands; and it provides a vast range of endeavor for the collector, the person who likes to gather and display items in which he or she has a great interest.

Origins of the Hobby

It all began several hundred years ago when people began fashioning replicas in miniature of the colorfully uniformed soldiers of the day. Later, they grouped them to re-create battle formations or scenes of combat. Around that time, craftsmen began to put together small models of sailing ships that ruled the seas. From the narrowest thread that rigged a mast to the carving on a deck cannon, the ship was magnificently formed in miniature. As time went on, new subjects presented themselves to the modeler. Almost as soon as a piece of equipment entered the military arsenal, it became a new stimulus for the modeler. Military aircraft were built in miniature almost at the same time that planes were introduced to battle in World War I. Tanks, jeeps and other vehicles were treated with the same acceptance by modelers as they made their appearance.

Today, there is an extraordinary selection of military items to model and collect. And there is practically no limit to where you can go in the hobby. Kits become increasingly complex; military figures are molded in ever-finer detail; displays and dior-

5

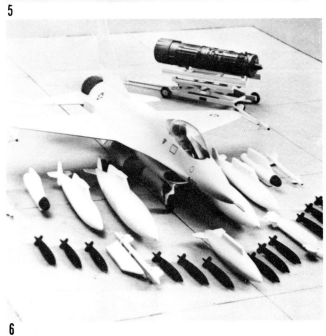

6

7

amas are never-ending challenges to the imagination and ingenuity of every modeler. You, the modeler, will find that the hobby shop has become your supply depot, your quartermaster corps, your recruiting agency. You can become the builder of armies, the general, the admiral, the designer of airplanes, the parade-master.

The joy and satisfaction of military modeling are experienced today by hundreds of thousands of people. This is a hobby that is not restricted by geography: it is something a modeler in the United States has in common with thousands of hobbyists in England, France, Germany, Japan—practically anywhere in the world today.

This book has several purposes. It is designed to take you on a whirlwind tour of what is available in the military modeling marketplace. It offers you a guide to getting started in the hobby and illustrates the work of experts. We offer chapters on all aspects of military modeling—soldiers, tanks, artillery, aircraft, ships, and military scenes.

Your chief interest may lie in collecting antique miniature figures, or in painting new figures so precisely that they will astound any onlooker. You may want to simply snap together the pieces of an inexpensive airplane kit because that particular aircraft is of significance to you, or you may decide to decorate it so realistically that it could win prizes in competition. You may be an amateur historian, a specialist of sorts in the saga of World War I, and wish to create three-dimensional illustrations of the battles you've studied.

MODEL MILITARY is designed to help you formulate your battle plan, to develop your strategy as you begin (or continue) your maneuvers through this exciting pastime.

Getting Started

1

THE FIRST step the military modeler has to take is to determine just where to begin. There are so many kinds of military models on the market today and they come in so many scales that it is enough to strain the imagination of practically everyone. Ships, tanks and other land vehicles, artillery pieces, aircraft and a vast assortment of military figures that range from spear-throwing warriors to present-day soldiers are available in dazzling variety. They include everything from simple snap-together kits for the beginner to models with hundreds of pieces for the expert. And there are sculpted, one-piece military figures that need only paint, but they can be as complicated and entail as time-consuming an effort as putting together any multipiece model.

The best way to acquaint yourself with what is available in military models is to pay a visit to your local hobby shop. The hobby industry has been growing steadily in recent years, and there has been special interest in the modeling crafts. The result is that a good, well-stocked hobby shop is not difficult to find.

Browsing in a hobby shop, you will quickly learn a lot about the military modeling world: what the different scales are, what technical guidebooks are available, how much individual items cost, what tools and supplies you have to choose from; and often you will find a display of models built by local experts that will give you an idea of just what you can accomplish with the hobby.

Beyond merely looking around the store, however, it is also wise to talk with the people who work there. Usually they are quite knowledgeable and happy to help. After all, if you are successful at the hobby and find it enjoyable, the shop will acquire a new customer. In addition, the people who own or work for a hobby shop often know of modeling clubs in the area, competitions or displays, and get-togethers of other modelers who might want to share their interests and expertise with you.

In the sources chapter in the back of this book, we describe some of the national organizations as well as the magazines that cater to the military modeler. Both can be a big help to the person just getting started in the hobby, and they are a source of continuing interest to the established modeler. It would be a good idea to get involved with these groups at the outset. The publications can be enriching because they are up-to-date on what is going on in the hobby and what new kits, tools, equipment and supplies are available. They also

2

3

4

Replicas of all types of war machines are made: those that travel under the sea (1), on the sea (2), on land (3) and in the air (4). The Polaris nuclear sub and USS Wasp aircraft carrier are from Revell. The 1:35 scale British Churchill Crocodile tank is made by MRC-Tamiya. Many modelers refer to packaging for paint details.

offer interesting articles and intriguing graphics on various aspects of modeling.

The kits you find in hobby shops come in boxes that should be sealed. This prevents you from looking at what is inside, but also helps ensure that the kit you buy will not have parts missing. The proprietor of the shop can tell you what the contents are like. In some cases, he may even have a similar kit that is already open so that you can examine the materials inside.

Unlike models of equipment or vehicles, military figures are often packaged in clear plastic bags. Therefore, you will be able to see what they consist of. Be sure to check whether any of the parts for the figures are damaged or broken. You can normally do this with nothing more than a simple visual inspection. In the case of a box or a bag that is not transparent, you will have to wait until after the purchase to examine the parts. Seldom will you find a broken piece inside a sealed box; but if you do, your hobby shop probably will replace the kit. Bagged items, on the other hand, are much more prone to damage in shipment and handling. If you are careful at the store, you may save yourself the trouble of a trip back to the shop later.

Boxes containing military model kits normally have full-color illustrations of the model on them. Sometimes it is a photograph of the model; more often, it is an artist's rendering of the vehicle or piece of equipment. This will be your most basic guide for painting and decorating the model. Therefore, you should be careful not to lose or throw away the box. In most instances, the illustration also will be a guide to creating a diorama. The item to be built is often shown in a realistic scene, or at least one that might provide various visual suggestions for placing the model in an authentic scene.

Scale and Size

Another important item on the box cover will be the model's scale. The model is a scaled-down version of a real piece of military equipment. In the modeler's language, the real thing is referred to as the prototype. The scale is the proportion of the model's size to that of the prototype. Scale is commonly expressed as a ratio like 1:72 or as a fraction such as 1/72. This means that one inch on the model represents 72 inches on the prototype.

Military figures, however, are not identified by scale. They are defined by exact height in millimeters, measured from the bottom of the foot of the figure to the top of the head. Any form of base, headgear, or hat is not included in the measurement. Therefore, a 25mm model soldier (which is one-inch tall) would be a true 1:72 scale model of a six-foot soldier as he would normally be measured from head to foot.

The scale of military models and the height of model figures are very important. If you are building a diorama or if you simply want to display models together, you will want all of them to be in the same scale. For the sake of authenticity, you would not want to position a model of a jeep in 1:24 scale next to a Sherman tank in 1:72 scale. The scale of a model is always clearly printed on the box.

In model railroading, letter designations are used to identify the scale of trains and environmental items. These scales—such as HO (1:87), S (1:64) and 0 (1:48)—can be useful to you as a military modeler, because you may want to use environmental items like these in a diorama or for decoration. You will have to be careful if you are buying items that are identified with a letter scale, however, because there are discrepancies. HO is a scale of 1:87 in the United States, but in Europe it is 1:76. Besides, most military models are not built to the most common railroad scales. Your best guide is simply to follow the numerical scale ratio on the box of the model you want to build. Anything you incorporate should conform to that scale.

Although most military models are manufactured within the range of 1:32 to 1:72 (1:48 and 1:72 being the most popular), the actual range can be as wide as 1:8 for a military motorcycle with sidecar to 1:500 for an aircraft carrier.

Prototypes are usually measured in linear feet. We speak of a 24-foot Panzer tank, for example, or a fighter plane with a 30-foot wingspan. The following chart can be helpful in calculating a model's size in relation to a particular prototype.

Model Scale	No. Inches to 1 Foot
1:500	.024
1:400	.030
1:300	.040
1:200	.060
1:160	.075
1:120	.100
1:96	.125
1:87	.138
1:76	.157
1:72	.167
1:64	.187
1:48	.250
1:36	.333
1:32	.375
1:24	.500
1:20	.600
1:16	.750
1:12	1.000
1:8	1.600

Aircraft models are available in many different scales, including 1:44 such as the Pocket Pak fighters from Entex.

Military figures, as we mentioned, are produced in varying heights. The most common today are 25mm and 54mm, but you will find a number of other heights as well. The following chart can be helpful in placing them in their appropriate scale. These are the five most basic heights of military figures:

Model Soldier Height	Equals in Inches	Scale to 6-Foot Man
12mm	.48	1:150
25mm	1.00 -	1:72
54mm	2.16 -	1:33
75mm	3.00	1:24
90mm	3.60	1:20

The Work Area and Tools

Good modeling is a hobby that requires organization and concentration. You will need the appropriate tools and supplies at your fingertips, and you will need an area where you can work undisturbed.

The work area should be one where you can leave your modeling for a while and return later without having to move the model or the parts you are working on. If you come home from the hobby shop and launch into building a model on the dining room table, chances are you will be disturbed at mealtime. If the model will take more than one day to complete—and most will—you should not be in a position where you have to pack up everything at the end of each day. If you have to do that, you run the risk of losing or damaging parts; having those that have been put together come apart or dry unevenly; or, even worse, have the glue set firmly with the parts not in their proper position.

Basements and family room corners are often preferred places to organize a work area. So are bedroom corners and garages. Any area that is out of the normal household traffic pattern and that can be maintained as a permanent model-building area is a good place. Each person's situation will be different, but you will never regret having planned and organized a suitable modeling area before starting work on the model.

The work area should include a large table or desk (the place where you will actually be working) and space for holding materials, supplies and tools. A pegboard wall or panel is easy to install next to or in back of your work table and it will provide an excellent place for hanging all kinds of tools so that they are easy to get to. A tabletop item that can also be quite helpful is a "scrap bin" to save all unused items (you may want to use them later on another model or in a different diorama). A cardboard box is all you need, but a drawer can serve the same purpose.

Because you will be working with glues and paints, it is wise to cover your work area with paper. The best kind of paper cover is heavy-duty brown

Hinchliffe's 70mm metal figure of the Italian Bersaglieri, expertly decorated by modeler Dave Fisher.

wrapping paper or the kind of paper that meat from the butcher shop is wrapped in. Not quite as effective, but still a very handy standby, is yesterday's newspaper. A paper surface, taped down while you work and simply discarded when you are finished, can save a lot of cleanup time.

All the parts of the model or military figure you have bought will be found in the container in which they are packaged. But the basic tools, adhesives, paints, and other supplies you will need will not be included. Fortunately, you can get by with a relatively small number of elementary items in the way of tools and supplies—at least at the beginning. As you move along in the hobby, however, you will undoubtedly want (and need) some more sophisticated tools and equipment.

The manufacturers of tools and supplies for the modeler are listed in the sources chapter in the back of this book. Many of them provide catalogs that illustrate the broad range of equipment that they make available to the modeler. Most of the items should be readily available at your local hobby shop. It is a good idea, too, when you are browsing for a model in a hobby shop to check out the various tools, materials and equipment on the shelves. In the hobby world, comparative shopping usually pays off.

We offer here a brief rundown of the basic tools and supplies that you will need as well as the extras. Remember, however, that what is basic to the beginner is not basic to the more advanced modeler. When we talk about the basics, we are referring to the items you would need to fashion a relatively simple model. What you are modeling and the degree of detailing, precision construction, decorating and painting you want to put into the operation will be the determining factors as to what you will need in the way of tools, equipment and supplies.

The Basics:

Hobby knife. These long-handled knives with a short, slanted, razor-sharp blade—the most familiar of which are produced by X-Acto—are very important because of the number of cutting, trimming and scraping jobs that they can do. You can substitute a single-edge razor blade for most of these jobs, but a hobby knife is much easier to use

and can be controlled much better. The knife should be purchased with a supply of blades.

Tweezers. These are needed for picking up, holding and positioning small parts during model construction and decorating. Be sure the gripping surfaces are not so rough that they damage or scratch what they are holding.

Sandpaper. You will need this to prepare surfaces for painting and to smooth areas or remove burrs or other unwanted protrusions. For finishing work on a model, you will want a fine sandpaper (Nos. 300, 400, or 500). For heavier jobs, you will need a rougher sandpaper. You can substitute an emery board for sandpaper in most instances, but be sure it is not too rough for the job.

Rubber bands. These can be used to hold glued parts together while they dry. For the same purpose, you can substitute masking tape, which works better on rounded surfaces, or spring clothespins.

Scissors. Common household scissors can be employed for a number of cutting jobs in modeling. Removing plastic parts from the sprues they are attached to, cutting out decals, and cutting paper

5

to cover work areas are just a few of the ways they can be put to use.

Toothpicks. Wooden toothpicks are excellent for applying small amounts of glue or cement or for putty work.

Modeling putty. You will find this form of putty ideal for filling holes or gouges, smoothing seams and contouring. Use the right kind; you will find it at your hobby shop and in most hardware stores. It can be applied by finger, dowel, toothpick, small spatula, or even screwdriver.

Modeling paints. Most hobby shops have large display racks of the various colors of paints specifically mixed for the modeler. The most well-known military modeler's paints come from Testor, Humbrol, Floquil, Pactra, Scalecoat, and I/R Paint Products. Colors are available for brush painting and spray painting.

Paint brushes. The quality of your painting is dependent in part on the type and quality of the brushes you use. Good sable brushes are less likely to shed hairs than are cheap brushes. The size of the tip of a brush is identified numerically, with the smallest beginning at 0 and progressing upward. A beginning modeler would do well to acquire an 001 (a very small tip), and a few larger brushes in the range perhaps of 1, 3, and 8. Look for quality: it's worth the extra money.

Miscellany. These are some things you may want (but not necessarily need) to have around: rags for cleaning; newspapers; an old, soft-bristle toothbrush for cleaning parts; cellophane or masking tape to hold parts or paper in place and for masking in painting; a paint solvent; and extra decals in case you damage the ones that come with your kit.

In addition to those basic items, there are others that are used by modelers, especially those who have progressed beyond the stage of beginner.

Needle-nose pliers. These can serve the same purpose as tweezers. Pliers also can be used for twisting and bending wires and for work over a flame.

C-clamps. This type of clamp, with its adjustable screw, is available at hardware stores and hobby shops. Excellent for holding parts securely so that they will dry evenly, C-clamps offer much finer adjustment than clothespins, rubber bands and tape. You will have to be very careful, however, so

6

7

No matter what scale you choose -- the 1:35 scale of MRC-Tamiya's U.S. armored personnel carrier (5), or the 1:48 scale of Monogram's B-29 Superfortress (6) and MRC's Fairchild Republic jets (7), the assembling of models will be most successful if you equip yourself with the proper tools and supplies.

Careful research results in models that are extremely accurate in detail, such as this Crusader III tank from Revell/Italaeri. This is why many modelers also become amateur historians.

that you do not damage the part being clamped; an extra turn or two of the screw can be trouble.

Vise. There are several kinds of vises available. Some can be fitted to your tabletop and become stationary items in your work area. Others are smaller and portable. Either type can be effective in model building because it can hold parts or sections securely, leaving your hands free.

Drills and gouges. These are specially made tools for work in modeling or other crafts that require tiny, precision-made holes. The drills, which ordinarily come with different bits, can provide exceptionally neat and precise boring, especially in areas where you are modifying parts or building from scratch.

Jeweler's saw. When you must cut through plastic, especially large or thick pieces, the jeweler's saw is about the best tool you can use. Clean, straight cuts are characteristic; but you may need to develop a little expertise in the use of this tool. At the beginning, try out your cuts on extra pieces of waste material until you feel you can control the saw well enough to get the precise cut you want.

Modeler's power tools. These are the top-of-the-line items in the modeler's tool kit. Power tools for the modeler come in a variety of forms and with varying accessories. The most well-known are produced by Dremel. These motorized tools can be used for drilling, carving, grinding, polishing, sanding, routing, engraving, cutting and detailing. They work well with plastics, wood, leather and even metal. A motor tool would probably be the single most expensive tool you buy for modeling. If you plan to truly work seriously at the hobby of modeling, it would be worth your while to investigate the different kinds of motorized tools and the accessories that are currently available.

Research and Construction

Inside the model box are all the parts of the kit you are going to build. At your work table, you have the tools, paints and other supplies necessary to carry out the job. You'll also have an instruction sheet that tells you step-by-step how to build the model. And you have the photograph or illustration on the box to give you at least a one-dimensional view of what the finished product should look like. But if you are really serious about modeling, that is not enough.

Authenticity and realism are the results of good military modeling. There are adaptations, refinements, modifications, embellishments—all kinds of things that a modeler can do to make his model a more authentic-looking one.

The best way to accomplish this is to find out more about the prototype. Some of the better model kits contain descriptive material about the prototype equipment, including its exact specifications. You can learn a lot just from carefully reading this before starting to build your model. However, you should search out different pictures of the prototype in real-life settings. There are many books devoted to military equipment, and some highlight models as well. Here, you can compare different colorings and detailings, the varying forms of camouflage and realistic weathering. You can work out in your own mind just what you want to show on your model and then determine how you can successfully do it.

Besides helping you in regard to authentic detailing, this research can help you create interesting and informative data sheets to go with your models. It also can provide material for all the necessary descriptions in a modeling "log book"—something many experienced modelers like to keep.

This, too, is another benefit of belonging to a modeling club. You can share ideas, experiences, even publications. The basic parts of a particular model are the same in every box, but the miniature replicas that are created from them are often very different because of what the modeler is able to contribute to it in terms of his skill and planning.

Once you have selected your model, set up your work area, organized your tools and supplies, researched the prototype, and determined what you want to do with your model, there is nothing left but to build it, paint it, detail it and display it.

The techniques that modelers use, however, are as different as the hobbyists themselves. The basic guide comes on a printed sheet in the box. Some items will have to be painted before they are assembled; others will have to be assembled separately, allowed to dry, and then joined to the model later. It all depends on the model. Each model has its own peculiarities, its own unique characteristics.

Therefore, the best thing you can do is read the instructions carefully and completely before starting Step 1. Then, plan your method of operation. Check to be sure that all parts are in the box and that they are free of damage.

The construction of a model is for the engineer in you. Painting and detailing, however, are for the artist within you. Almost everyone can put together a model with a little help from an instruction sheet. But not every beginner can do a good job in finishing it—which includes painting, detailing, and decorating the assembled model. Here is where experimentation, practice, and experience play important roles.

Paintings prepared by the artists at Peerless models serve as a guide to modelers who strive for great authenticity in their replicas: details of camouflage, for instance.

Military Figures

1

MODEL SOLDIERS, military figures, toy soldiers—all are names that have been attached to tiny replicas of soldiers that have been collected by hobbyists for more than two centuries. Over the years they have been produced in paper, wood, metal and plastic. They have represented warriors from ancient civilizations; the tribal hordes of the Dark Ages; the knights and crusaders; and the cavalry and infantry that fought in all the wars of Europe, Asia and the United States during the last several hundred years.

The earliest traces of model soldiers go back to around 2000 B.C. when Egyptians carefully carved figures from wood and placed them in tombs. As time went on, miniatures were fashioned to serve utilitarian purposes. Military strategists positioned them in battle formation to plan real battles. It was an operation very similar to today's wargaming; but in those days, it was no game.

In the late 1700s, the hobby of collecting military figures spread to the "common" people of Europe. Previously, it had been the domain of kings, generals and the very wealthy. In those days, the army officers of Prussia, Austria, France and England were outfitted in resplendent uniforms. It was natural that miniatures of these handsome figures would be created.

In Germany at Nuremberg, and in France at Strasbourg, craftsmen established successful businesses of producing inexpensive models. The first model soldiers were printed on paper that was to be cut out and fastened to pieces of wood. These were popular; however, in the days of quality materials and great pride in workmanship, they proved less than durable. So flat models on wood and metal were formed and then hand-painted. It was also possible to buy the flats unpainted so that the hobbyist could decorate them himself.

The next stage brought about one-side molding of models, which produced detailed relief features

2

3

4

Military figures are made in metal and in plastic, and either kind can be decorated by the modeler or simply collected. Monogram makes figures in 1:35 scale (1) that can be painted to suit a variety of scenes. Metal "flats" are still sold under the Ochel name (2). The Britains company makes plastic figures (3) today, and made hollow metal ones (4) prior to World War II.

on one side but a reverse side that remained flat and undecorated. These figures are often called semi-rounds, but many modelers refer to them simply as flats, even though they are unlike the true flats that preceded them.

Once it was evident how lifelike these molded models could be, it was not long before craftsmen began fashioning fully rounded models. The first of these began to appear in France in the years just after the French Revolution. A sculptor in Paris began molding them in lead, and their popularity quickly spread to England and Germany. Later, tin and an alloy of tin and antimony were used.

From that time on, military figures were commonplace as collectibles and toys, pursued by everyone from hobbyists to antique collectors. Today, model soldiers are still molded in metal—painted and unpainted—and many are cast in plastic. And the hobbies of modeling and collecting them are as strong as ever.

Modeling and Collecting

Military figures, much more than other types of military models, offer a distinction in many cases between modeling and collecting. All modelers are collectors, but not all collectors are modelers. Some people search out antique miniature soldiers and extremely well-crafted modern models and purchase them completely finished. Their satisfaction is in the ownership and display of the models. Miniatures also are collected for the purpose of investment because collections of model soldiers have been sold for thousands of dollars. If this is where you want to direct your efforts, you will have to research and study what to look for in antique and rare models. As there are for other areas of collecting, there are books devoted to the collection of antique toy soldiers and models, and there are experts and dealers you can consult.

In this book, however, we are primarily interested

in the modeler who paints and decorates his own miniatures. Here is a pastime that offers opportunities for the highest caliber of craftsmanship in modeling and an extremely broad range for imaginative display.

On today's market, you will find expertly defined moldings in metal as well as plastic. Plastic kits are also available which require you to put the model together and enable you to select the pose of the figure. Fine metal models like those from Stadden, Imrie/Risley and Hinchliffe, and top-quality plastic ones such as those put out by Polk/Heller or Historex have superb detail. You can achieve excellent results in decorating them, as you can see from the models shown on the following pages.

The range of soldiers to model is practically endless. Traditionally, the most popular are the elaborately uniformed men of the Napoleonic era—French, Prussian and English—as well as those of the years just before that time. Modern-day soldiers are also popular, especially those from the two world wars. The internationally recognized size is 54mm (exactly 2.16 inches)—measured from the top of the model's head to the sole of the foot, regardless of headgear or stand. This is a scale of

about 1:32 or 1:33. You will find that these are the most abundant models on hobby shop shelves today. However, 25mm is increasing in popularity, especially with wargamers, and 75mm has long been collected by modelers.

Modeling soldiers can become a rather costly hobby: it is habit-forming; there are thousands of figures to decorate and collect; and the opportunities for dioramas are limited only by your imagination, your ability to conduct basic research, and your budget. Metal models today, depending on their size and detailing, range from about $3.50 apiece to just over $15. Plastic kits range from as little as $1 up to about $6. You will need a large assortment of paints and an adequate supply of good paint brushes for this branch of military modeling.

Once you are involved in modeling soldiers, you will be re-creating the history of men in war, those who fought the great battles from Waterloo to Bastogne, from Prussia to Gettysburg, from the Punic Wars to the battles of the Sinai Peninsula.

British 16th Lancers. Cavalry battles were a part of just about every war up to World War I. This dio-

rama (5) depicts the horsemen of the British 16th Lancers, a proud regiment of about 1846. The first lancers can be traced back to the ancient Assyrians and Egyptians. Later, they were immortalized by the medieval knights. Russian, Polish and French lancers were effective in the Napoleonic Wars, so much so that the British organized similar regiments shortly after observing them in battle. The British continued to use them in battle as late as 1898. In fact, the lance as a weapon was not formally retired from service in the British Army until 1927, although it had not been used for more than 25 years.

This diorama was made from three separate kits produced by Historex, each of which was converted (the modeler's term for modifying or adapting) to create the positions of horses and men in this original scene. The figures and horses are plastic, in the 54mm scale.

Washington's Bodyguard Corps. Elegance in uniforms was not restricted to European officers and soldiers of the 18th and 19th centuries. In America as well, members of the military decked themselves in colorful and handsome uniforms, as shown by this depiction of a member of General George Washington's Bodyguard Corps (6). The Bodyguard Corps was, however, at one extreme of the American fighting men of that war. They were well-trained soldiers, equipped and uniformed as such, who guarded the general and also fought as regular front-line soldiers. At the other extreme were the equally patriotic volunteer militiamen who often had no official uniform, only the most rudimentary equipment and little or no training.

This model of a Bodyguard Corps soldier comes from Imrie/Risley, cast in metal at 75mm scale.

Greek and Roman Soldiers. Ancient warriors were not as regally uniformed as many of the later European and American military men, but their outfits were unique and historically significant. The Greeks had Alexander the Great and his conquests, and the famous Peloponnesian Wars between Athens and Sparta as part of their military history; the Romans had their Caesars, their empire, and the Punic Wars with Carthage.

Ancient Greek and Roman soldiers are represented in the three models here (7). The figures are molded in plastic by Atlantic in HO scale (1:87), the

6

7

Beautiful examples of the modeler's art: (5) diorama created by Commander Terry Barton (MC) U.S. Navy; (6) Washington's bodyguard created by Ken Boyle; (7) Greeks and Romans painted by Skip Peterson.

19

8

9

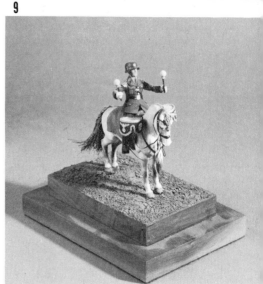

10

most common scale used by model railroaders but a relative rarity in the hobby of modeling figures.

French Carabiniere. The Napoleonic Wars produced some of the most dazzling of uniformed figures—the Prussians alone had hundreds of different, richly adorned uniforms for the various troops from its different states and provinces. Russia, Austria, England and especially France were not to be outdone either in that period of elegant warfare. This model (8) is of a French *carabiniere,* a mounted rifleman from the period 1807-1815, the age of the Napoleonic Wars. He is a trumpeter as well. Napoleonic figures have long been the most popular models to build and collect. Literally hundreds are available and the opportunities for conversion are limitless.

This plastic model, in 54mm scale, was assembled and decorated from precise directions provided with the kit by Historex.

Israeli Female Soldier. Modern military personnel are almost as popular with modelers today as are the colorful Napoleonic and Prussian officers. The young woman represented by this model (9) from

Squadron/Rubin is an Israeli soldier, trained and prepared for combat just as the male soldiers of that country are. Today, women play a large and important role in the nation's armed forces. The model here was cast in metal in 54mm scale.

SS Kettledrummer. In the modernized and mechanized German military forces of World War II—a country known for *blitzkrieg* tank attacks and V-2 rockets—a horseman seems somewhat out of place. But Adolph Hitler liked the pageantry of military parades and great military rallies. Horsemen, like this model of an SS Kettledrummer, provided much of the pomp and ceremony before and in the early years of the war. By 1944 and 1945, however, as Germany went on the defensive, all the bandsmen, horsemen and other ceremonial types were marshalled into the *Wehrmacht* and *Waffen SS* armies to fight rather than to perform.

The model shown here (10) is actually a combination; the kettledrummer is from a kit produced by Segom, and the horse is from Historex. It is modeled in plastic in the 54mm scale.

British Private (commemorative). As handsome in

Pvt. Loading
1879

11

12

uniform as they were well-trained, the members of
Britain's 24th foot regiment were a proud lot. This
model (11) is actually a commemorative of a particular soldier, a private from the second battalion
of that regiment who fought and was killed during
the Zulu War in southeast Africa in 1879. The private was encamped near a place called Rorke's
Drift with more than 800 other British soldiers and
almost 500 African support troops when they were
surprised by an attack of a Zulu army of almost
10,000 men. All but a few British and African de-
fenders were killed. The survivors retreated to
Rorke's Drift. Along with the small garrison there,
they held off six more attacks by the Zulu army.

The minimen model is metal in 54mm scale.

Kaiser Wilhelm. Kaiser Wilhelm II, emperor and
king of Prussia from 1888 to 1918, was resplendent
in a wide variety of elegant uniforms—from the tip
of his *Pickelhaube* (the traditional German spiked
helmet) to the toes of his gleaming black boots.
Modeled here (12), however, he is wearing a *Garde
du Corps* uniform with an eagle replacing the spike
on his *Pickelhaube*. Kaiser Wilhelm was a true
military leader—a commissioned army officer as

well as a head of state. But he lost his ruling power
over Germany even before the German offensive of
1918 collapsed. He then fled into exile in the Neth-
erlands, where he lived until 1941.

This metal model from Superior Models is one of
the largest you will find in today's marketplace, cast
at 90mm scale.

British Seaman. Seamen with the British Royal
Naval Brigade, like the one represented by this
model (13) from Cameo Personalities, were land-
fighting men as well as sailors, like the U.S. Marines
of today. This rugged seaman would have fought in
the Boer War, which is more formally known as the
South African War, about 1899 or 1900. Raids were
common for heavily armed seamen (note the band-
oliers), who participated in numerous hit-and-run
attacks on the South African coast.

The model is metal and cast in 80mm scale. No
converting was done here; the model was decorated—quite skillfully—as it came from the manufacturer and according to the detailed painting
instructions included with the model.

Coldstream Guard. Among the most colorful of

21

13

14

15

16

More excellent figures: (13) British seaman from Michael Cobb; (14) Coldstream guardsman painted by Bob Bihari; (15) Napolean and friend by Ken Boyle; (16) Mackensen by Pete Kailus (also shown unpainted).

British military units, in terms of the uniforms they wore and their long and distinguished history, is the Coldstream Guard. Recognized by their ornate headgear, these foot soldiers marched and fought through more than two centuries of British battles.

The Coldstream Guard was officially formed on St. Valentine's Day 1661 from Oliver Cromwell's Lord General's Regiment of Foot Guards as a special unit to protect King Charles II of England. The Guard later grew to a much larger infantry force. Under the command of General George Monck, 1st Duke of Albermarle and one of Britain's most famous military leaders, the Guard originally head-quartered at Coldstream near Berwick-upon-Tweed in Scotland, and took its name from that town almost immediately upon its formation and commission. The Coldstream Guard adopted the motto *Nulli Secundus* — second to none — and proved it appropriate by its actions in battle during the next several hundred years.

This Coldstream Guardsman of 1815 (14) is fashioned from a plastic model manufactured by US Airfix. It is in 1:32 scale.

Napoleon Advancing. All military miniature scenes do not have to depict combat or military ceremony, as this setting (15) imagined in the parlor of some early 19th century palace in France, amply illustrates. The man is Napoleon Bonaparte; the woman is unidentified. The kit from Phoenix Miniatures, which includes both figures and the sofa, is appropriately entitled "Napoleon Advancing."

There are numerous examples of military men in nonmilitary dioramas that you can obtain today or devise yourself by converting various models. Over the years, these little scenes have ranged from the serenely domestic through the mildly suggestive to the downright scandalous. Although this 54mm model depicts what is probably a fictional scene, it is known that Napoleon did not spend all of his time on the fields of battle or in the halls of government.

Prussian Field Marshal. One of Germany's most famous military figures was Field Marshal August von Mackensen.

In World War I, Mackensen successfully led the German troops in battle against the Russians at Brest-Litovsk and Pinsk and later against the Serbians and the Rumanians in other battles. His career was equally colorful before the war. In 1869, to begin his military career, he joined the 2nd Death's Head hussars, an elite cavalry unit. He rose to the rank of regimental officer, and finally to the general staff level. Depicted here (16) in the uniform of the Death's Head hussars in 1910, he held the rank of colonel and chief commander of the unit. After that, Mackensen went on to take command of the combined Prussian/Austrian 11th Army.

Field Marshal Mackensen is commemorated here in this large-scale 80mm metal model, a product of Superior Models.

Land Weapons:

Armor and Artillery

Extraordinary realism: diorama featuring U.S. Army halftrack, created by modeler Dave Elliott.

THE INFANTRY moves on its feet—at least in the past it did. In today's modern army, it gets some help from trucks, armored personnel carriers and helicopters. And it receives assistance in battle from a number of other military divisions. Armor, artillery, logistical command, support; the transport of soldiers, of equipment and supplies, or arms and ammunition—all are equally important factors to the military forces of the world.

The tanks, cannon, missile launchers, half-track, jeeps and motorized guns constitute some of the most interesting and exciting models in the world of military miniatures. There is a broad range to choose from, stretching from the earliest pieces of equipment that maneuvered on the battlefields of a time long since past to replicas of those that are part of today's most modern armed forces.

When we think of armor, we usually think of tanks. And that often brings to mind World War II and names like Rommel, Patton and Montgomery. The scenes these devastating vehicles can summon up are dramatic, to say the least.

In the mind's eye, one person will see German and British tanks driving across the barren desert of North Africa, churning up sandstorms as they converge in battle. Another person might conjure up the scene of long columns of Panzer tanks rumbling across the European countryside that they have just conquered. Someone else would picture American tanks noisily rolling over the cobblestone streets of Paris to the cheers of the French people they helped to liberate; Russian tanks lined up as a great land armada, raining heavy artillery barrages on the bunker in Berlin as the last few

1

2

square feet of Third Reich territory falls to the Allies.

Armor, however, isn't just tanks. It encompasses a wide variety of military vehicles plated with armor. These range from tanks to numerous kinds of personnel and artillery carriers. And armor, which we so often associate with World War II because of its extensive use and impressive accomplishments during those bloody years, is by no means limited to that war. Armor has, in fact, been an integral part of armament from World War I to the recent wars in Vietnam and the Middle East.

Modelers have always been particularly fascinated with armored vehicles for two reasons: the prototypes have an exciting and romantic history in battle; and fully fashioned, well-rendered models of them stand out as artful and dramatic creations. To be convinced of the popularity of models of armored vehicles, all you have to do is look at the shelves of a hobby shop. There you will find a wide and ever-increasing range of kits and collectibles of these kinds of items, offered by many of the most well-known names in model manufacturing, such as MRC-Tamiya, Polk/Heller, Monogram, GHQ, Peerless, Minicraft, Otaki and ESCI.

The kits offer the potential for fine model making. Generally speaking, the materials are of high quality. But there is another important consideration. Research, as we mentioned earlier, is one of the greatest tools of the serious military modeler. This is especially true with armor. These pieces of equipment have an abundance of unique details and other identifications. The basics of the prototype may be included in a kit, but there is a broad area for individual effort to make the models more authentic and more exciting.

A Short History of Armor

The tank is an awesome symbol of military power, and it is the one we most often associate with armor. Heavy, powerful, fast, maneuverable, armed with everything from heavy artillery pieces and machine guns to devastating flame throwers — the tank appears to be an indestructible weapon. It can attack, pursue, or serve as a stationary fortress.

The tank as we know it today was actually born in World War I. It was introduced by Britain and first used in warfare by that nation at the battle of the Somme in 1916. But the principle of the armored vehicle can really be traced back to the armored war chariots that were used in early Roman battles. Even Hannibal's elephants were protected by a coat of armor and, in their own way, were armored personnel carriers.

Armored cars actually preceded tanks. Back at the turn of the 20th century, they were being experimented with in England. Early types consisted simply of armor plates and a turret to house some form of gun. They saw little use in the trench warfare of World War I, however.

During World War I, tanks were used only sporadically by the British and French. The Germans didn't employ them until 1918; and then most of the ones they used had been captured from the British or the French. Tanks were simply not very important weapons in that war; they were still in their experimental stages.

Among the best known of the World War I tanks was the British Mark I (actually the first tank used in battle). It weighed 31 tons, paltry by today's standards. It carried two six-pounder pieces of artillery and four machine guns. The French also produced

3

Tank kits from Revell: (1) StuG IV Assault Gun in 1:35 scale; (2) snap-together rocket launcher tank; (3) Sherman M4A1.

two well-known tanks, the Renault and the St. Chamond, both named for the companies that produced them. They were smaller and had considerably less firepower (usually only one to three guns) than the British Mark I tank, but they were durable and maneuverable vehicles that served effectively.

By the end of the war, Germany turned out its first large tank, the A-7V, built by the famous automobile maker Gottlieb Daimler. (Daimler later founded the company that manufactured the Mercedes-Benz automobile.) His tank was powerful and heavily armed (a cannon and six machine guns) and was manned by a crew of 18, but it came along too late to have any appreciable effect on the course of the war.

In the United States, Ford Motor Company and various tractor manufacturers set out to copy the British and French tanks. The results were some small versions of these European tanks that were used in training in the United States (under the command, incidentally, of a lieutenant colonel named Dwight D. Eisenhower), but they did not reach the battlefields of Europe before the war came to an end.

Experimentation continued during the years between the two world wars. The emphasis then was on smaller, lighter tanks for use with infantry units. The United States turned out two important tanks during that time, the 23-ton M-2A1 and the 14-ton M-2A4, which were the prototypes of heavier tanks that were to be produced for use in World War II. Development and testing of a wide variety of other armored vehicles also got underway in the U.S. as well as in Europe.

It was not until 1938, however, that the design,

production and utilization of armored vehicles really got moving. The British, French, Germans and Americans all realized the effectiveness of the tank and the armored car as decisive factors in battle. They therefore set about arming themselves accordingly.

Germany alone turned out more than 40,000 tanks during the first five years of World War II. Perhaps the most famous of all the German tanks was the Panzer, a 47-ton monster that could travel at speeds of up to 30 miles an hour. It was a very effective piece of armored equipment and was produced by the arms manufacturers of Germany in a variety of sizes for different functions in battle. After the Panzer, the German Tiger was perhaps the next most important piece of armored equipment in the Axis forces. It was larger than the Panzer and had heavier firepower. It, too, was adapted for different types of warfare.

Britain countered the Germans with the Churchill and the Cromwell, two heavy-duty tanks, and the Comet, a speedy lightweight. But the United States provided the true thrust of combat when it turned out almost 50,000 M-4 tanks. This vehicle later became better known as the Sherman tank. The Shermans combined exceptional artillery and machine gun firepower on a tank that could operate over the worst of terrain and in the foulest of weather conditions. Great speed and excellent maneuverability made the Sherman tank a model for all succeeding U.S. tanks.

The U.S.S.R. produced the T-34, a medium tank, and the huge KV (more than 52 tons).

Following World War II, tank design and equipment continued to improve. In the ensuing years, the United States made good use of the powerful 46-ton M-60, which became the official tank of all NATO forces. The U.S.S.R. came up with powerful and fast tanks they called the T-54 and the T-62. And Israel used the U.S. Patton tank, the M-48, with great effectiveness in the desert wars of the 1970s.

The tank, motorized armored artillery, armored personnel carriers and other armored vehicles are important weapons in the arsenals of all countries. The range of models, as you will see on the following pages, is almost as extensive and diverse.

Jeep and Artillery. Ernie Pyle, America's most famous news correspondent during World War II, once wrote, "Good Lord, I don't think we could continue the war without the jeep." He was certainly close to the truth: hundreds of thousands of these vehicles were used for an extraordinary number of purposes in that war. The jeep was actually designated as a quarter-ton truck by the Army, the smallest of military trucks used in World War II. But the jeep took officers, non-coms and enlisted men where they had to go; it transported ammunition, supplies, and equipment; it served as an ambulance, fire truck and police car.

Jeeps were seen rolling out of amphibious land-

4

5

Among the many tanks produced by the U.S. and its Allies during World War II were the British Churchill Crocodile (4) and the Russian assault gun (5). Both models are made by MRC-Tamiya. Other ground vehicles of World War II included the U.S. Jeep (6), from Monogram, and the German armored car (7), from MRC. Also produced by MRC-Tamiya is a model of a postwar West German tank, the Leopard A-4 (8). The Leopard was introduced in the mid-1960s.

ing craft into the surf of an invasion beachhead, or being parachuted into battle zones. The four-wheel drive of this pugnacious vehicle enabled it to go almost everywhere in the worst of weather conditions and terrain, and it could achieve speeds of 60 miles per hour on the road. Jeeps have been part of the United States military transportation system ever since that war.

This model (6) illustrates the typical army jeep of World War II. It is a plastic model from Monogram, in 1:35 scale. The two soldier figures and the piece of light artillery come with the kit.

German Armored Car. The armored car is almost as old as the automobile itself. Back in England in 1899, the development of armored cars began when a man named F. R. Simms took a powered quadricycle and equipped it with a machine gun. A year or two later, he added armor to its body, and the armored car was born. There was no real need for them, however, until World War I broke out in 1914. Armored cars were used to a degree in that

war, but they could not function off the road, and that is where most of the trench warfare took place. Experiments with ways to get armored cars to operate effectively in the fields and over difficult terrain is actually what led to development of the tank.

During World War II, the armored car was brought into battle when the German Panzer units used them for a variety of attack support activities. Vehicles like the German 222 shown here (7) were used extensively both in the desert warfare of North Africa as well as the combat zones of continental Europe. This particular version of the armored car had four-wheel drive and four-wheel independent suspension. It carried a 20mm gun in the car's turret, and could be driven at speeds of up to 56 miles per hour. This replica is from MRC-Tamiya, made of plastic in 1:35 scale. The uniformed figure is included in the kit.

West German Leopard A-4. The West German Leopard tank was the first postwar tank to be built in Germany. It was commissioned after West Ger-

6

7

8

many became a member of NATO, and the first new Leopard tank was introduced in 1966. It is a highly improved version of the German Leopard used during World War II. Today's Leopard tank is designed for duty in continental Europe and has been exported to various NATO nations. The new tank is a big one, weighing about 40 tons and reaching a length of over 31 feet. It can travel at speeds up to 40 miles per hour and has a range of more than 375 miles. The first of the new Leopard tanks were armed with one 105mm cannon and three 7.6mm machine guns; newer versions carry a variety of different weapons modified for specific functions.

The model shown (8) is from MRC-Tamiya, fashioned in a large 1:16 scale in metal, which can be built either as a static model or one that is radio-controlled. The basic model features movable turret, hatches, machine gun and periscope. Radio-control versions are designed to be used with two-channel digital proportional radios. RC kits are provided with gearbox, clutch and motors already assembled. These motorized models will move for-ward, in reverse, turn to the left or right, and climb inclines of up to 40 degrees. The kit also includes some tools for working with the metal parts, and even some transmission grease.

U.S. Truck Tractor and Semi-Trailer. The "Dragon Wagon," as it was known in World War II, was specially developed to haul tanks from one place to another. Sometimes it was quicker and easier to haul a tank to a battle area than it was to drive it there. In other situations, it was necessary to transport a damaged tank back to where it could be repaired. To handle this difficult operation, the U.S. Army Ordnance and the Pacific Car and Foundry Company developed the 12-ton M26 Truck Tractor and its companion piece, the 45-ton M15-A1 Semi-Trailer unit. They were introduced to the battlefields of World War II in June 1943. Soldiers watching this equipment haul huge tanks back and forth came up with the name Dragon Wagon. The cab of the Truck Tractor was heavily armored so it would be functional under heavy battle conditions.

Among the machines used to haul supplies and weaponry were the U.S. "Dragon Wagon" (9) and the "Jimmy" (10). **10**

The entire unit was capable of transporting a load of 40 tons.

The multipart model shown here (9) is plastic in 1:35 scale and includes three uniformed figures. It is a product of Peerless.

Army Cargo Truck. Early in 1940, the United States began adapting a standard commercial truck so that it would function as a standard military truck, capable of meeting all the specialized requirements that that would present. The result was the basic 2½-ton cargo truck developed by General Motors which featured a rear cargo carrier that could be adapted for a variety of transportation purposes. The most common sight, however, was the one depicted by this model (10) with the familiar canvas canopy and the silver-white star on the door. The truck was given the nickname "Jimmy."

It had four-wheel drive, which enabled it to be operated in snow, ice, mud and sand. The canvas-covered cargo compartment was used to transport everything from armed troops to supplies, equipment, ammunition, and practically anything else a combat force would need in the way of support. The truck could easily be converted to a flatbed and be outfitted with containers for transporting water, fuel, or other liquids. More than 800,000 of these 2½-ton cargo trucks were produced during World War II—a mass-production effort that is impressive by any standards. This highly detailed model, which features an AA machine gun and crew, is from Peerless. It contains 144 parts, including those for the two uniformed figures. The model is plastic and molded in a scale of 1:35.

M4 Sherman Tank. The core of U.S. armor in World War II was the famous M4 Sherman tank, which fought in all theaters of the war from 1943 until the German and Japanese surrenders in 1945. A total of more than 48,000 M4 Shermans were produced during the war. They were an especially crucial element in the advance across France and Germany during the war's last years.

The Sherman did not have the firepower of some other tanks, like the German Tiger, for example, but it had an exceptionally mobile turret that gave it an advantage in battle. Its original armament included a 76mm cannon, a 12-inch mortar, and three machine guns; later versions incorporated different guns. The Sherman had a top speed of about 30 miles per hour and a range of 120 miles. It was not especially heavy—just short of 34 tons—but it carried a 62mm thickness of armor. After World War II, the Sherman tank was kept on active duty and served as the standard tank of NATO forces. It was used effectively by the United Nations forces in Korea and also by the Israelis in the Six-Day War of 1967.

The model shown here (11) is a specialized version called the M4 Sherman "Hedge Hog," complete with a gouging bumper up front and sandbags. The model is from Monogram. It features movable guns and comes with a uniformed figure. It is plastic, in 1:32 scale.

Anzio Annie. No country in the history of warfare utilized the railroads and railroad systems more than Germany did in World War II. Europe had a magnificent railroad transportation network, and the Germans took excellent advantage of it—in some unique and startling ways, as shown by the model here of the famous "Anzio Annie" rail gun (12). This particular gun was actually named the Leopold; it was nicknamed Anzio Annie by American soldiers landing at Anzio, Italy, in the early months of 1944, who felt the effects of its heavy bombardment.

11

The United States' M4 Sherman tank, when equipped with a gouging bumper, was known as the "Hedge Hog."

12

The huge gun was transported by rail to a position for firing, which could be as far as 30 to 35 miles away from its target. The huge 70.67-foot barrel would handle a 550-pound, 11-inch shell, making it one of the most powerful pieces of artillery used during the war. The Leopold was captured by U.S. soldiers in Italy after the Anzio landings. It was preserved and brought to the United States after the war. Today it is housed at Aberdeen Proving Grounds, Maryland, and is open to public display. This model, fashioned in plastic, is from Minicraft/Hasegawa and is rendered in a scale of 1:72. The kit also includes the railroad bed and stand on which Anzio Annie is displayed here.

U.S. M3 Lee Tank. Before the United States entered the war with Germany in World War II, U.S. military experts knew that the army needed a highly maneuverable, medium-size tank to counter the German Panzers. After a lot of study, experiment and

testing, a new and radically different tank came into being. Instead of the traditional single turret, the new piece of armor had three turrets and was equipped with a truly impressive array of armament—so much weaponry, in fact, that it was nicknamed the "Moving Fortress." But the Army formally named it the M3 Lee, after Robert E. Lee, commander-in-chief of the Confederate Army.

Its arsenal of weapons included a large 75mm tank gun at the right side of the hull, a 37mm tank gun in the lower left turret, and a revolving 7.62mm Browning machine gun in the top turret. The tank also carried four 30-caliber Browning machine guns. Capable of speeds in excess of 30 miles per hour, the 28-ton tank could negotiate inclines of up to 31 degrees. The M3 Lee fought at El Alamein in North Africa and the Battle of Tunisia. More than 6000 M3s were produced before they were replaced by the famous M4 Sherman tank. This plastic model (13) is from MRC-Tamiya, in 1:35 scale.

13

14

15

"Anzio Annie" painted by Cy Broman (12); models decorated by MRC -- Lee tank (13), and U.S. halftrack (14, 15).

U.S. Armor Half-Track. Both the United States and Germany developed half-track vehicles for use in World War II. They were used for basic transportation and as armored combat equipment. The United States began building them as far back as the late 1930s, and the various models were continually improved throughout the war. The last (and best) version was the M3A2, represented by the models shown here (14,15). Hard-faced armor, varying in thickness from 6mm to more than 12mm, provided protection for the vehicle. As many as 12 fully armed soldiers—the equivalent of a full squad —could be accommodated in this vehicle. The M3A2 was outfitted with a variety of weaponry: usually a .50-inch Browning anti-aircraft machine gun, a 2.36-inch rocket launcher (or bazooka), and various smaller machine guns; plus a supply of hand grenades, mines, and other explosives.

Half-tracks were used in Europe and in the Pacific during all of World War II. The United States produced more than 45,000 half-tracks during that war. Most were vehicles similar to the model shown here—those designed as armored personnel carriers—but about 8000 of the total were actually self-propelled pieces of heavy artillery. These models in plastic, are from MRC-Tamiya in 1:35 scale. They contain approximately 120 parts, and also include nine uniformed figures.

German Tiger. In early 1941, Adolph Hitler directed the building of a heavy, powerful tank to combat the large, new tanks being employed by Russia and Britain. The German firm Henschel began work and soon came up with a tank that was to become known as the Tiger. It was one of the heaviest tanks of its time, and a unique one at that, being the first of its kind to utilize overlapping wheels. It also carried the largest single piece of artillery of any tank in operation, an 88mm gun, which could penetrate a four-inch plate of armor at 1600 yards.

17

16

German Tiger tank from MRC-Tamiya (16), United States Patton tank from Monogram (17), antitank gun diorama created by Bill Larides (18).

18

The first of the Tiger tanks were sent to the eastern front to fight at Leningrad. The cold gray of their original paint blended in with wintry Russia. Subsequently, desert camouflage like that shown on this model (16) was used when the tanks took an active part in the war in North Africa. Because of its great artillery power, the Tiger was one of the most destructive tanks ever produced up to that time, and it was especially effective in standoff battles with other tanks. The Tiger was also used as a standard defensive weapon in 1945 when the war had moved to German soil. But the crews were mostly replacements, and Allied power by that time had become overwhelming. A later version, the Tiger II, was built to even larger proportions, weighing out at 68 tons, to become the heaviest tank to fight actively in World War II.

The model shown here is of a Tiger I that went to war in the desert. It is a plastic model in 1:25 scale from MRC-Tamiya.

Patton Tank. Named for the most famous tank commander of all time, General George S. Patton, the army's M47 appeared shortly after World War II. It weighed out at 44 tons, heavier than the M4 Sherman, and carried more powerful armaments: the Patton tank was outfitted with a mighty 90mm cannon as well as various machine guns. A crew of five was required to man the tank. Its range was only 100 miles, less than that of the earlier Sherman, but it could traverse the distance at speeds up to 37 miles per hour.

That speed would have impressed General Patton, because he was known to squeeze every last bit of speed from the tanks under his command. That was one of the reasons why he was able to get to Bastogne in time to rescue the American troops

surrounded by the Germans there in the winter of 1944-1945. The Patton M47 distinguished itself in battle during the Korean War. It was also exported to many NATO nations for use in their armies.

The model shown here (17) is from Monogram, formed in plastic at a 1:32 scale.

Artillery Scene. Artillery has been a part of war since the Middle Ages, when armies first fashioned catapults to hurl stones and flaming debris at their enemies. Since that time, artillery has played an important role in one form or another in every war. Shot and shell replaced stones, and the strategy of using these devastating weapons of war was refined to a science. The cannons of the past were eventually replaced, too, this time with mortars and howitzers. In World War I and even more so in World War II, artillery had to be designed not only for use against troops and defense barriers but also against armored war vehicles and aircraft.

Specialized light artillery, like the 75mm German antitank gun shown in this scene (18), was developed as countries were producing huge howitzers capable of hurling 200-pound explosive projectiles over distances of 15 to 20 miles—and doing it with pinpoint accuracy. Today, surface-to-air and surface-to-surface missiles and rockets have added a new potency to the artillery stockpile.

The scene depicted here is a typical one from World War II, when artillery was so crucial to halt the advance of marauding tanks. The 75mm antitank gun is a plastic model from MRC-Tamiya, molded in 1:35 scale. The figures are German artillery soldiers of the *Grossdeutschland* Division, rendered in plastic at a scale of 1:35 by US Airfix. The stand and groundcover were made from scratch.

Sea-Going

War Machines

1 *Imai's Greek Galley kit, built and decorated by modeler Joseph Oppenheimer.*

SHIP MODELING is one of the oldest hobbies in the world. Over the years, replicas have been fashioned from wood, ivory, whalebone and stone. In ancient times, carefully crafted boat models were placed in tombs to carry the spirit of the deceased on its journey to the afterlife. Some models have been assembled inside bottles. Others have been used for experiment and planning before actual military battles; in fact, complete scale models of invasions, including the cliffs, trees and shrubbery, and exact shorelines as well as all the boats and ships involved were often created in World War II for use by the U.S. Navy.

In the museums of the world, there are probably more models of historic or classic sailing ships than any other military-type model. The reason is that ship modeling can be incredibly intricate, involving elaborate webbings, sail configurations,

and minute detailing, sculpting and engraving. And much of the work is scratch building. Some of the finished models of these ships of yore, most of which were military ships, command several thousand dollars, if, of course, the hobbyist is willing to part with a model he has worked on for perhaps two or three years.

Elaborate ship models that come in kit form are designed for the advanced modeler. To complete them you will need tools, experience and skill, patience and ambition. These models are something to aim for in modeling; the resulting replicas are true showcase items. In this chapter, however, we'll discuss models of more modest demands, the kind that the beginner or relatively inexperienced modeler would want to get involved with.

There are many plastic and some wood and metal kits available today—models of everything from PT boats to gigantic aircraft carriers, from historic ships to modern nuclear-powered vessels. The kits are put out by companies such as Monogram, MRC-Tamiya, Otaki, US Airfix, Valiant, Heritage Models and Revell. They are relatively inexpensive, but they have the potential to be turned into handsomely decorated scale models.

Scale presents some problems for the military ship modeler. Huge vessels like aircraft carriers with 1000-foot flight decks cannot be fashioned in the same scale as a jeep, because the ship model would be far too large to be practical (or the jeep would be far too small). So scales for the big ships like the carriers, battleships, and heavy cruisers often are in the range of 1:350 to 1:700; some can go to 1:2500. Therefore, you will have to adjust your displays to accomodate this. Many military modelers simply display their naval miniatures apart from other models that are built to different scales.

Because of the size, number of parts and amount of detailing required, ship models involve a lot more time and effort than other military models. The results, however, can be spectacular, depending on the amount of detailing you do and the proficiency you have in finishing the model.

What you can expect to model in this area are a variety of military ships including galleons, privateers, square-riggers, clipper ships and other men o' war of the past; other historic ships like the Monitor and Merrimack; those that composed the vast naval forces of the United States, England, Germany and Japan during World War II; and those that make up present-day armadas.

A Short History of Warships

Military vessels can be traced all the way back to the ancient civilizations of Egypt, Phoenicia, Crete, Greece and Rome. Between 2000 and 500 B.C., oar-powered ships ruled the Mediterranean Sea. Galleys, as they were called, often had masts and sails but were still powered primarily by slaves pulling at the oars. They were used mainly for carrying warriors.

As time went on, ships got larger—as did the armies that needed to be transported. The Vikings of Scandinavia built their own longboats, which could transport about 60 soldiers each. They were also pointed at bow and stern and therefore could be used to ram other vessels.

The Middle Ages, however, was a great era for sailing ships. By the 1400s, large ships with several masts and many sails used the wind and the principles of sailing to replace the muscles and oars of slaves. Gunpowder and cannons were used to arm the warships. Ships could thus do battle on the high seas and therefore control all transportation by water.

The caravel came first. It was a three-master, with the largest mast up front. Although they were not warships, Christopher Columbus' Nina and Pinta were caravels. Other caravels were outfitted with cannons. After the caravel came the galleon, made famous by the Spanish and Portuguese.

In the 1600s, the frigate was introduced. A light, fast and well-armed fighting ship, it was in a way the forerunner of the destroyer and the cruiser. Larger ships—with two, three, or even four decks, each armed with cannons—were the "line" ships. They carried many sails and were the battleships of the day. The corvette was also a battle craft; it was smaller than the frigate and had less powerful artillery. Corvettes were used for various assault and hit-and-run operations.

Ships grew in size, complexity, speed and firepower. England, France, Spain and Portugal all vied for mastery of the seas. Square-riggers and heavy frigates carried complements of 60 or more cannons. Great names of fighting ships began to emerge: Admiral Horatio Nelson's flagship at the battle of Trafalgar, the Victory; the U.S. heavy frigate of the Revolution, the Constitution; later the sleek clipper ship Cutty Sark.

Like the oar, however, the sail too passed into obsolescence for warfare. Steam engines, which had been experimented with for years, were finally perfected for realistic use by Robert Fulton when he put them to use to power the Clermont down the Hudson River. The modern military warships evolved from there.

In World War I, warships transported troops and battled on the sea. Submarines, destroyers, light and heavy cruisers as well as a variety of smaller boats and landing craft were employed by both the Allied forces and the Central Powers. Near the end of the war, the first aircraft carrier made its appearance. It was the English carrier Argus.

World War II was as much a naval war as it was a land and air war. All we have to do is think back: the devastation of the Pacific Fleet at Pearl Harbor; the great battles of Midway and Leyte Gulf; the U-boat action in the Atlantic; the great invasions of the Pacific islands and Europe; the transportation of troops, arms, equipment and supplies.

Today, nuclear-powered ships roam the sea— over the waves and beneath them. Ships and submarines are armed with nuclear warhead missiles and other incredible firepower. Giant aircraft carriers with the ultimate in space-age equipment and computerization handle supersonic jet airplanes and are, in effect, floating cities.

Whether your interest as a military modeler is in past history—the romance of the galleons, frigates and clipper ships—or in the awesome power and might of the naval vessels of today, you will find models in kit form so that you can recreate them in miniature. Just what can you accomplish as a relatively new military modeler? Just look at the pages that follow.

USS United States. One day in July 1797, the frigate USS United States was launched at the

2

4

3

5

naval boatyard in Philadelphia. It was the first of three fast, well-armed warships that were destined to become famous. By autumn of that year, the USS Constellation and the USS Constitution ("Old Ironsides") filled out the new armada.

Nicknamed "Old Waggon," the USS United States distinguished itself in battle first against privateers and later during the War of 1812. Classified as a 44-gun frigate, the USS United States was actually armed with 52 cannons: thirty 24-pounder guns were mounted on the gun deck; twenty-two 42-pounders were housed on the forecastle, quarterdeck, and on the deck amidships. Because of its array of weapons, it was known as a "double-banked" frigate. All of this made the USS United States the most heavily armed frigate on the high seas when it was first launched. It was also quite large for a frigate, measuring 173 feet in length and just over 44 feet at its widest point. Like its sister ship "Old Ironsides," the USS United States earned a high place in the annals of U.S. naval history.

The model shown here (2) is from Revell, molded in plastic at a scale of 1:96. Revell's model features preformed billowing sails; rigging cords; well-detailed gun, spar and poop decks; a ship's wheel;

three cutters; two jolly boats; a launch; a dinghy; and 20 crew figures.

HMS Bounty. The HMS Bounty is one of the most famous ships ever to take to the sea. Its fame does not stem from battles that it won or lost, but from the most publicized mutiny in all of naval history. The story of the Bounty has been told often in books, major motion pictures have been made about it, and students of naval history still argue about the mutiny.

It all occurred in April 1789, when the HMS Bounty was sailing near the Friendly Islands not far from Tahiti in the South Pacific. Master mate Fletcher Christian led a mutiny and seized the ship. Captain William Bligh and 18 members of his crew were set adrift in a longboat. In this tiny open craft they managed to travel almost 4000 miles across the Pacific to the East Indian Island of Timor, near Java. Christian took the Bounty to Tahiti and then Pitcairn Island where he set the ship on fire. Christian founded a colony on Pitcairn and Captain Bligh returned to England to take command of various other British warships.

This model of the famous Bounty (3) is formed in

plastic at a scale of 1:150. The manufacturer is Lindberg.

HMS Victory. On October 21, 1805, England's most famous admiral, Horatio Nelson, stood on the quarterdeck of the HMS Victory off Cape Trafalgar in the Atlantic just south of Cadiz, Spain. His ship was then involved in one of the most famous battles of the Napoleonic Wars—in fact, one of the most significant conflicts in the history of all naval warfare. A sharpshooter in the crow's nest of the French ship Redoubtable sighted Nelson and fired his musket. The admiral was hit, and was taken below. Nothing could be done for him, however, because the bullet had severed Nelson's spine. He died a few hours later, a short time before the English won a complete victory in the Battle of Trafalgar.

The HMS Victory had been Admiral Nelson's flagship, and it was a ship worthy of that honor. It was a "ship of the line," as they were called in those days, a forerunner of today's battleships. Ships of the Victory's type had been the principal and most effective fighting ships on the high seas since the days of the Spanish Armada more than 200 years earlier. The Victory was a magnificent example of a ship of the line. It was 186 feet long and weighed more than 2100 tons. Each of its three decks was armed with cannons, and its three masts carried eight huge sails. The HMS Victory survived all its battles and all the hostile seas it sailed. It is preserved today for display in the naval dockyard at Portsmouth, England.

There are a number of models of the Victory currently available in kits of varying degrees of complexity. This model (5) is from Lindberg. It is made of plastic in a scale of 1:350.

USS Hornet. The USS Hornet played a prestigious role in the early days of battle in the Pacific during World War II. As an attack aircraft carrier, it was one of the most important pieces of naval equipment in that theater of operations after the devastation of Pearl Harbor. The Hornet—along with other carriers like the Yorktown, Enterprise and Saratoga, and a few other small warships—were all that were left to carry on the war for the United States after Japan's disastrous bombing raid on Hawaii.

From the deck of the Hornet, Lt. Colonel Jimmy Doolittle launched his famous B-25 raid on Tokyo in 1942. The Hornet brought the bombers to within 500 miles of Japan, where they took off from the carrier, dropped their bombs and continued on to landing fields in China. And the Hornet was one of the crucial factors in the United States' victory in the Battle of Midway, one of the war's most important naval combats. At the end of October 1942, however, the Hornet was badly damaged in the Battle of the Santa Cruz Islands, just east of Guadalcanal; its crew was evacuated and the carrier had to be scuttled so that it did not fall into enemy

hands. In its brief wartime service, the Hornet proved the importance of the aircraft carrier in modern warfare.

This model (6) is rendered in plastic at a scale of 1:700, and is a product of MRC-Tamiya. Because aircraft carriers are very popular with military modelers, there are many others to choose from besides the Hornet, including everything from the large Japanese carriers of World War II and other famous U.S. carriers of that time to the modern nuclear-powered carriers of today.

Scharnhorst Battlecruiser. In the early years of World War II, the Germans controlled the waters beneath the Atlantic Ocean and the Mediterranean Sea with their force of deadly U-boats. They tried to do the same thing on the surface, building their power for the most part around a core of three fast and powerful ships: the battleship Bismarck, and the battlecruisers Gneisenau and Scharnhorst. The Bismarck was the largest and most famous of the three ships, even though it did not survive the spring of 1941. Both of the smaller German battlecruisers outlived it to fight in many other naval battles, but they were never able to take control of the surface waters of the ocean. The aircraft carriers, battleships, and destroyers of the combined United States and British forces were much too powerful.

6

7

USS Hornet diorama decorated by John Waite (6), Scharnhorst battlecruiser built by Ralph Muscente (7), Monogram's Bismarck (8) and USS Enterprise (9) shown in action.

The Scharnhorst is referred to as a battlecruiser rather than a battleship because its function was somewhat different: it was designed to be a faster, lighter-armed, and lighter-armored vessel than the heavy battleships of the day. It was capable of speeds of more than 31 knots and its weight was just short of 32,000 tons. Housed on the ship were nine 11-inch guns in three turrets—two at the bow and one at the stern. Other lighter pieces of artillery were placed on the sides of the ship.

The extremely well-detailed model shown here (7) is from MRC-Tamiya, rendered in plastic at a scale of 1:700.

The Bismarck. In the shipyards of Germany in 1936 when work began on the huge battleship Bismarck, the word was that the ship would be unsinkable. The fast, heavily armed battleship would carry such incredible armor plating, it was said, that nothing would be able to bring it down. It was being plated with a complete sidebelt of armor, 12½ inches thick at the lower level and 5¾ inches thick around the upper area. The deck also carried a 4-inch armor plate, and below deck an allegedly unique system of internal subdivision would enable areas to be sealed off in the event of an emergency to prevent flooding.

When it steamed into battle in World War II, the Bismarck seemed to be every bit as invincible as its builders had claimed. Capable of speeds of 30 knots, the 42,000-ton battleship carried eight huge 15-inch guns as well as an effective variety of smaller artillery and anti-aircraft guns. When it faced the new British battleship, the HMS Hood, in May 1941, the Bismarck blew the Hood out of the water. But the Bismarck also had to do combat with another battleship, the HMS Prince of Wales, and an aircraft carrier in the same battle. The Bismarck was damaged but escaped the combined attack—at least for the moment. A day or so later, however, aircraft from the carrier HMS Ark Royal tracked it down and sent torpedo after torpedo at it. The great ship floundered but did not sink. Then other British ships joined the attack and the combined forces of sea and air power finally sunk the unsinkable Bismarck.

The replica of one of the world's most famous warships shown here (8) is from Monogram. It is fashioned in plastic and features turrets that turn and guns that can be elevated. No scale is noted, but the completed model measures 16 inches in length.

USS Enterprise. The longest warship in the world today is the nuclear-powered aircraft carrier USS Enterprise. Its deck is 1123 feet long, the length of

8

9

almost four football fields laid end to end. It was also the heaviest warship on the seas at 74,700 tons until the launching of the carrier USS Nimitz, which weighs in at 91,400 tons.

The Enterprise was the first nuclear-powered surface warship. Construction of the Enterprise was begun in 1958; the ship was commissioned in the U.S. Navy in late 1961. It has been on active duty ever since. Eight nuclear reactors power turbines to drive the ship's four screws, and atomic power has proved efficient: after it was launched, the Enterprise cruised more than 207,000 miles over a three-year period before it had to have its nuclear reactors refueled. The Enterprise, which is capable of carrying as many as 100 aircraft and is itself armed with nuclear missiles, is one of the most important elements in the present-day American naval arsenal.

This model (9), which is only one of many replicas of this famous ship currently available, is made by Monogram. It is molded in plastic at a scale of 1:400. Included in the kit are 40 aircraft, deck tractors, helicopters, missile launchers, and a display stand.

U-boat. The scene is a familiar one. A long convoy of ships silently zig-zags across the ocean. On its perimeter, destroyers patrol the waters to protect it. But beneath the waves, a submarine captain sights through his periscope and gives the order to fire torpedos. Moments later, one of the merchant ships explodes in flame and then sinks to the bottom of the sea.

In the early days of World War II, there was nothing more fearsome than the marauding German U-boats—the scourge of the Atlantic Ocean, as they were called—which continually prowled for merchant ships, tankers and warships to destroy. If one U-boat was lucky enough to spot a convoy, its captain would alert other U-boats in the area and they would gather for what became known as "wolf-pack" attacks. Hundreds of Allied ships were sunk by U-boats in the first years of the war—some within sight of America's east coast.

The history of the German U-boat actually goes back to World War I, when submarine warfare was first waged. Only about 60 U-boats, however, were on or under the water at one time during that war. During World War II, Germany built more than 1100 U-boats, but 785 were destroyed in battle. The invention of radar and sonar during the war and the improvement of U.S. antisubmarine weapons and tactics turned the tide of battle against the German submarines midway through the conflict. This model (10) is of the World War II German submarine U-107. The model is in plastic, manufactured by Nichimo in 1:200 scale.

PT 109. PT boats were small, exceptionally fast, maneuverable boats designed for quick torpedo attacks in World War II—especially on merchant ships. They were also used for patrol duties in the Pacific Islands. PT is an abbreviation for Patrol Torpedo.

The most famous of all PT boats is PT 109, not so much because of what it accomplished or the battles in which it was involved, but because its commander was John F. Kennedy. Under Ensign Kennedy, PT 109 was on patrol in the Solomon Islands in the southwest Pacific when it was rammed by a Japanese destroyer. PT 109 sank, and Kennedy and 11 members of his crew swam three miles to the closest island where they were rescued several days later.

All the PT boats used during World War II were lightweight craft with no armor, but they carried torpedos and light naval artillery weapons. PT 109 is typical of the thousands of small attack boats that played important parts in the overall combat efforts of the U.S. Navy in the Pacific.

The model shown here (11) is from Revell. It is molded in plastic, and the kit comprises 12 pieces and a display stand. No scale is listed, but the completed model measures 13¼ inches in length.

USS Arizona. On December 7, 1941, more than 100 Japanese airplanes streaked from the sky over Hawaii and zeroed in on the U.S. naval base at Pearl Harbor. Among the most vital U.S. ships based there were the heavy battleships, which formed the

10

U-boat model by Nichimo in 1:200 scale (10).

11

Revell's model of John F. Kennedy's PT 109 (11).

core of the U.S. Navy's Pacific attack fleet. The USS Arizona was one of them. It, along with 85 other ships anchored at Pearl Harbor, was caught by surprise in the Japanese raid. The Arizona was destroyed in the attack, and it was sunk, taking with it many of its crew and entombing them beneath the sea.

Seven other battleships were also severely damaged in the attack, as were other ships and boats in the port. A total of 177 U.S. airplanes were also destroyed. More than 3000 men of the U.S. Navy and the army were killed in the sneak attack. Fortunately for the United States, its aircraft carriers were at sea that day in December and were saved. The rest of the Pacific fleet, however, was severely crippled by the major losses at Pearl Harbor and would not be able to get back into good combat shape for more than a year.

At Pearl Harbor today, a huge concrete structure has been built over the Arizona's bridge to stand as a monument to all the Americans who died in the attack.

The model shown here (12) is plastic, manufactured by Revell. It is authentic in detail, but has no scale designation. It comes complete with its own two-piece display stand.

USS Constitution. Moored in the shipyard in Boston Harbor today is one of the most famous ships ever to sail under the flag of the United States. The USS Constitution—better known as "Old Ironsides," a nickname it received as a tribute to the staunchness of its oak side-paneling—is on display for people who wish to see what a fighting frigate was truly like. "Old Ironsides" participated in and won 40 naval battles. It fought against French privateers around 1800, against the Tripolitain pirates in the first few years of the 19th century, and was best known for its impressive victories over English warships during the War of 1812.

The construction cost was less than $303,000 for this mighty frigate, which was 204 feet long, 43½ feet wide, and carried an arsenal of more than 50 cannons. The copper sheathing on the bottom of the ship was specially made for it by one of the world's most famous horsemen, Paul Revere. "Old Ironsides" remained in service from its launch in 1797 until 1828. It was kept in drydock for 100 years and then restored so that it could take its place among the most impressive of American monuments.

This model (13) from Revell is rendered in plastic. No scale is noted for the model, but when finished it will measure 16 inches. The kit features one-piece mast and spars, sails, detailed ratlines and thread, and a display stand.

USS Halsey. Today's navy depends on weaponry different from the seagoing forces of World War II. Missiles with nuclear warheads are an integral part of many ships' arsenals. They are still supple-

12

13

14

Paintings of USS Arizona (12) and USS Halsey (14) at war; Revell's "Old Ironsides" (13).

mented, of course, with conventional artillery and anti-aircraft guns; but nowadays, most types of ships, from aircraft carriers to nuclear-powered submarines, are outfitted with devastatingly powerful missiles and nuclear warheads.

The USS Halsey, the model shown here (14), is a guided-missile frigate. It is very similar to a destroyer in size, armament, and military function. Like destroyers, frigates are fast, geared to similar kinds of naval in-fighting, and they are especially effective as attack vessels and antisubmarine craft. Frigates, like destroyers, in the United States Navy today are named for famous naval and marine heroes of the past.

This frigate is named for Admiral William "Bull" Halsey, commander of America's 3rd Fleet in the Pacific during World War II, who guided the U.S. naval operations in such famous battles as Guadalcanal and Leyte Gulf. This model of the USS Halsey is plastic, a product of Monogram Models. No scale is designated, but the finished model will display a 16-inch hull.

Military Aircraft

THE HOBBY of building model airplanes has been with us just about as long as the airplane itself. In fact, building miniature, developmental model aircraft goes back long before the Wright brothers got their flying contraption airborne back in 1903. Designing and constructing those kinds of miniatures was not a hobby in the 1800s—the models were experimental tools of dreamers and serious inventors—but once planes proved they could be flown, people immediately saw the excitement and glamor attached to these incredible machines. The hobby of fashioning detailed replicas of them was born and grew quickly.

Among the most interesting pieces of aircraft to model are military airplanes. They are specially designed and elaborately equipped; they require precision detailing; and they offer dramatic displays when complete. There are many different kinds of military aircraft to choose from—each with its own intriguing history.

If anyone questions the romance associated with military airplanes, all they have to do is think back on the nerve-shattering duels in the sky over the battlefields of World War I, when pilots like Manfred von Richthofen (the "Red Baron") and Eddie Rickenbacker—even Hermann Goering—maneuvered their open-cockpit biplanes and triplanes in deadly combat. Think of the dog-tired pilots of World War II trying to land their crippled planes on the deck of a heaving aircraft carrier, or bringing a bomber back on a single engine and the last few fumes of gasoline.

Few will forget Pearl Harbor; the German blitz of Britain; Hiroshima and Nagasaki; the U-2 spy planes; the raid on Entebbe. Practically every nation in the world today has its own air force.

For the modeler, there is a great range of kits on the market—replicas of hundreds of different pieces of military aircraft. It is almost possible to re-create from kits the entire history of military aircraft of the United States, Germany, Japan and England. And for the more popular models—the P-38s of World War II, the Fokkers of World War I, or the F-4 Phantom jets of today—there are a number of scales to choose from as well as kits that offer widely ranging levels of complexity.

If you have been an airplane modeler, you've been a military modeler. Many airplane model builders are specialists who are not at all interested in creating miniatures of tanks, battleships, Grenadier Guards, or military dioramas; they restrict their military modeling only to building such things as German Stukas, Russian MiGs, or U.S. B-29s. The military modeler, on the other hand, is interested in

MRC-Tamiya's model of the Avro Lancaster (facing page); Monogram's Avenger TBF (1), Dornier Do17Z (2), F-80 Shooting Star (3) and Messerschmitt Me262 (4).

model military aircraft as part of his overall military modeling efforts. Combat airplanes are combined with other weaponry to represent military history.

Scale is as important a consideration with model planes as it is with other military models. A large number of scales is available. Generally speaking, model airplanes are commonly found in the range of 1:24 to 1:72, with the preponderance of kits in the same scales as most other military models (1:36, 1:48 and 1:72). You may have to do some hunting for a particular model, however, if you want it in the same scale as other military models you have.

Like other models, airplane kits come with the basic ingredients in the package but require you to provide the art supplies, equipment and tools. No lifelike military aircraft is spotless. Your model, if you want it to look realistic, will have to be decorated to make it look like a real combat plane and not one that has just come off an assembly line. Research into photographs of the aircraft in real-life situations can provide all the guidance you will need.

Military aircraft can be displayed in many ways. Beyond the traditional shelf display or shadow box, they can be hung, mounted on a base, or incorporated into a diorama.

A Short History of Military Aircraft

Military aircraft were used long before the airplane came into existence. As far back as the French Revolution in the 1780s and 1790s, balloons were used for reconnaisance missions. In the next century, balloons were supplemented with kites, and later with gliders. During the American Civil War, balloons were used by the Union armies to send men up to determine the location and strengths of Confederate forces.

After the Wright brothers moved the world into the aviation age, airplanes were looked upon as having at least the possibility of service in the military—not necessarily as a weapon, but perhaps as an instrument for scouting or spying on an enemy and for transportation.

World War I started people thinking that aircraft had greater potential for military use. Among the first pieces of equipment during that war to extend the range of aircraft to actual combat activity was the German Zeppelin—a rigid, lighter-than-air aircraft. This dirigible and others, mammoth balloon-like machines as long as two football fields, were used both for reconnaisance and for bombing raids on land and at sea.

The airplane made its battle debut over Europe in

World War I. The war at that time was still primarily a land war, fought in the trenches and fields with infantry, artillery, and some armor. The airplane was an important factor, however. Fighter planes and bombers were developed by both sides and were used effectively. As early as 1915, a ship was sunk by an airplane that dropped a torpedo and scored a direct hit. The United States garnered a force of more than 2000 airplanes to augment the grand offensive of 1918.

Soon, aircraft names like Fokker, DeHaviland, Gotha, Spad, Boeing, Nieuport and Sopwith Camel became well-known to all men fighting the war in Europe. Battles raged in the skies for the first time in the history of warfare—plane against plane in what came to be known as dogfights. Similar battles would be repeated many times in the wars to follow, with single-engine biplanes replaced by jets.

It was during World War I that many of the first steps were taken in modern aerial warfare: the first aircraft carrier was built; formation flying was developed; strategic bombing was introduced to modern combat. By the end of the war, however, the generals who led the ground armies and the admirals who commanded the forces at sea were not convinced that the airplane was more than a sometimes handy gadget for locating the enemy. Wars were won by conquering land and controlling the seas, they argued. This type of reasoning prevailed after the war (which is why Colonel Billy Mitchell was eventually court-martialed and was removed from the U.S. Army when he fought for the creation of a separate air force and criticized officers who opposed the idea).

As the airplane was improved, becoming a faster and more versatile piece of equipment, its potential became obvious. And by the time World War II began, every nation knew the value of fighter planes and bombers in every aspect of battle: dive bombers; strafers; torpedo carriers; long-range bombers; transporters of paratroops, equipment and supplies. The military airplane had become an essential piece of military hardware. Germany had its *Luftwaffe* with more than 5000 aircraft and about 500,000 men. The English had their Royal Air Force, composed of about half that number of aircraft and a fifth that number of men. The United States had formed the Army Air Corps (the U.S. Air Force did not become a separate branch of the armed services until 1947) and the Navy Air Corps. The two comprised about 6000 usable airplanes. By the end of the war five years later, the United States had produced and used approximately 200,000 military aircraft.

Single-wing planes had replaced the old biplanes and triplanes. The power source range was from single-engine fighter planes to multi-engine super-fortress bombers. And at the very end of the war, jet aircraft made its appearance when the Germans introduced the Messerschmitt Me 262.

Germany turned out a devastating array of fighter planes in the early years of the war: Stukas, Mes-

5

7

6

Included in Revell's line of World War 1 biplanes and triplanes are: the Spad XIII in 1:72 scale (5), Baron von Richtofen's Fokker Dr. I in 1:28 scale (6), and the Albatross D-III in 1:72 scale (7).

serschmitts, and Focke-Wulfs. Japan had its Zero and Raiden. Britain countered with its famous Spitfire; the United States had the P-51 Mustang, the P-47 Thunderbolt and the Grumman Avenger to name only a few. Light bombers and combination fighter-bomber-interceptor airplanes bridged the gap between the fast, maneuverable fighter planes and the huge bombers. Heavy strategic bombing was a major factor in World War II. It began with the Boeing B-17 and grew with the B-24s and superfortress B-29s—the latter delivered the atomic bombs to Japan.

After World War II, the jet-engine airplane replaced propeller-driven aircraft in most military arsenals. Along came the Russian MiGs and the U.S. F-4 Phantoms, F-86 Sabrejets and the F-16s and the F-104s. Huge bombers like the B-47s and B-52s were capable of carrying huge loads of bombs thousands of miles—feats that were unheard of in the past. Helicopters became a major instrument of battle, especially in Korea and Vietnam. Transport planes became larger and faster than ever before. Rockets and guided missiles became part of the armaments of aircraft. Tanker planes could refuel bombers in flight. Jet fighters could be catapulted from aircraft carriers.

The military airplane has come a long way, from the Fokker Triplane with a maximum speed of only a little more than 200 miles per hour to supersonic jets that can fly 10 times that fast. Examples of nearly all of them are available in kit form.

Israeli Mirage 5J. The Mirage 5J fighter-bomber, which has distinguished itself as an important factor in Israel's air force, is produced by the French aircraft manufacturer Le Groupe Dassault Breguet. The same aircraft has been sold to the armed forces of France, Belgium, Libya, Venezuela, Peru and a number of other countries. It is Israel, however, that has used the single-seat jet in actual battle. The Mirage is not only fast (maximum speed of 1460 miles per hour), but it is also capable of carrying a 2000-pound bomb load or a devastating combination of bombs and missiles. It can fly at 40,000-foot altitudes.

This plastic model (8) is from Revell, in a scale of 1:32. Featured are a hinged cockpit canopy that can be opened, a detailed cockpit with ejection seat and pilot, a full set of decals, two Sidewinder missiles, four bombs and two rocket pods.

Grumman F6F Hellcat. From mid-1943 until the end of World War II, thousands of Grumman F6F Hellcats took off from the heaving decks of U.S. aircraft carriers. Hellcats were the primary carrier fighter planes during that period for both the United States Navy and the Marine Corps. At the time, they proved to be the finest carrier-borne fighter planes ever developed. In fact, of the almost 6500 enemy aircraft shot down by aircraft carrier pilots in all of World War II, 5156 were credited to the pilots of Grumman Hellcats. The single-engine, single-seat fighter was capable of a maximum

8 *Revell also makes models of modern aircraft, including the Israeli Defense Force's Mirage 5J.*

9

10

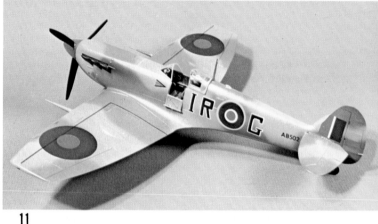

11

speed of 380 miles per hour, its power produced by a 2100-horsepower Pratt & Whitney engine. The plane's maneuverability and climbing power also contributed to its superior effectiveness in combat with Japanese aircraft.

The F6F Hellcat has long been one of the most popular aircraft to be modeled, and kits are available from quite a few model producers. This particular model (9) is from Monogram, molded in plastic at 1:48 scale. It is pictured here with Monogram's 1:48 scale model of the Thunderbolt P-47D.

Messerschmitt BF-110C. The name Messerschmitt was associated with a variety of highly effective German *Luftwaffe* airplanes in World War II. The BF-110C (10), was a two-engined, two-seat fighter-bomber, very similar to the earlier Messerschmitt Me110. Capable of long-range flying, these planes were used for fighter cover and precision bombing through most of the war, at least until Hermann Goering's *Luftwaffe* fell apart in the last two years of combat. German fighter bombers like these were used effectively in the blitz bombing of Britain in 1940 and 1941.

The airplane is named for Willy Messerschmitt,

the aircraft engineer who designed it and who also lent his name to other important planes in the German air force. The Messerschmitt Me109 was a heavily armed fighter plane that was very fast: in 1939 it held the world speed record of 435 miles per hour. It ranked with the finest aircraft made for World War II. Messerschmitt also developed the first jet-fighter aircraft, the Me262A, which was produced in limited quantities at the end of the war, and the Me163 Komet, the first airplane specifically designed for a liquid-fuel rocket engine.

The BF-110C model shown here is from Fujimi, rendered in plastic at 1:48 scale.

Spitfire. The Spitfire, a fast, exceptionally maneuverable fighter plane, was one of Britain's two answers to the German *Luftwaffe's* Messerschmitts and Focke-Wulfe fighters. (The other famous British fighter was the Hurricane.)

This plastic model (11), in 1:32 scale from Minicraft/Hasegawa, is of the Spitfire Supermarine MKVB, which was developed later in the war as an improvement over the highly effective Spitfires that took part so ably in the Battle of Britain in 1940 and early 1941. The single-engine, single-seat Spitfire

12

Grumman Hellcat, shown with Thunderbolt P-47D (9), Messerschmitt painted by Leo Bouché (10), Spitfire decorated by Dick Warfel (11), and Monogram's Russian MiG-15 (12).

Supermarine had a top speed of about 400 miles per hour and was considered by many to be the finest interceptor-attack plane to have fought in World War II. It joined the Lockheed P-38 Lightning, and later the North American P-51 Mustang and Republic P-47 Thunderbolt, to provide the finest fleet of bomber escorts ever developed. The Spitfire was also used on occasion to chase down and destroy the unmanned V-bomb rockets that Germany launched at Britain from across the English Channel.

MiG-15. Air combat in the Korean War was reminiscent of that in World War I—dogfights—but the newer planes were jets and they could attain a speed of about 600 miles per hour. The North Koreans flew the MiG-15, the newest jet fighter plane from the Soviet Union in 1950. The MiG-15 is represented here (12) by a model from Monogram.

In the skies over the Korean peninsula, the MiG-15 was opposed mainly by the F-86 Sabre Jet, an American-made plane flown by United Nations forces. Many aviation experts said the MiG-15 was the finest jet fighter plane in the air during the early 1950s. Besides the exceptional performance capa-

bilities of these airplanes, the MiG-15 pilots had an additional advantage during the Korean War: they could meet in a dogfight or take part in a raid and then flee northward over the Chinese border where they would not be pursued by U.N. aircraft. Despite all this, the MiG-15 could not dominate air warfare in Korea. Their pilots were not as well trained as the American pilots who flew the Sabre Jets. (By the end of the war, the score was a confirmed 838 MiG-15s shot down in air-to-air combat by F-86 pilots, and only 114 F-86s destroyed by MiG-15s.

This plastic model is made in a scale of 1:48. A pilot figure comes with the kit.

Sopwith Camel. Up to 1917, Germany had pretty much ruled the skies of World War I, dominating it with Fokker and Albatross airplanes. All that changed, however, when the British introduced the Sopwith Camel and the French developed the Nieuport and the Spad (which Eddie Rickenbacker flew with enough proficiency to become a WW I air ace). All were fast, dependable fighter planes that could compete admirably with the best that Germany had to offer. The Camel—which derives the first part of its name from the Englishman whose firm devel-

45

Captain Roy Brown's Sopwith Camel -- credited with shooting down von Richthofen in a World War I dogfight (13).

oped the airplane, Sir Thomas Octave Sopwith—was a faster airplane than those Germany sent up against it and could be handled easily in any type of aerial dogfight. The Sopwith Camel was used to test the launching of fighter planes at sea. Camels would take off from a barge that was being towed behind a destroyer. There was some thought given to using the barges as a force to protect naval convoys, but aircraft carriers soon proved that they could do the job more effectively.

The plastic model shown here (13) is from Revell, molded in a scale of 1:28.

F-4E Phantom II. One of the most versatile modern-day planes is the U.S. long-range fighter-bomber, the F-4 Phantom II, built by McDonnell-Douglas and used by the air force and the navy. Capable of taking off and landing on aircraft carriers as well as conventional airstrips on land, the

F-4 Phantom II (along with F-105 fighter bombers and the Strategic Air Command's B-52 Stratofortress heavy bombers) was instrumental in the bombing forays of the Vietnam War in the late 1960s. The Phantoms are heavily armed. They can fly at speeds up to 1450 miles per hour, at altitudes of 36,000 feet, and for a maximum range of about 1860 miles.

This model (14) is of the U.S. Air Force's F-4E Phantom II, manufactured by Revell. The U.S. Navy's counterpart is the F-4 Phantom, also available as a Revell model. Both are plastic models in 1:32 scale. The F-4E model here (14) features movable wheels and tailhook; a removable turbojet engine; three removable fuel tanks; canopies hinged so they can be opened; a detachable nose cone; detailed cockpit and instrument panels; movable landing gear; two crew members; and an arsenal of weaponry that includes four Sparrow missiles, six 500-pound bombs, four Sidewinder heat-seeking missiles, and a 20mm Vulcan cannon in the nose of the plane.

Stuka Dive Bomber. The way they could attack and the sound they produced as they dived at the enemy made the Junkers JU87 Stuka Dive Bombers formidable in their ability to strike terror in the troops they strafed and bombed. The German *Luftwaffe* used Stukas in a wide range of air combat activities, but the planes were hampered considerably because their top speed was only 210 miles per hour—not very fast compared to the 400-mph British Spitfires and the equally fast U.S. fighter planes. The Stuka was most effective when it was used against infantry and armor because it was difficult to shoot down with land-based anti-aircraft guns when it dived. In flight, however, it was highly vulnerable to interceptors, other attack planes, and to anti-aircraft fire. The Stukas sustained very heavy losses during the Battle of Britain in 1940 and 1941, and by the end of the war they were virtually wiped out.

The plastic model from Revell shown here (15) is a JU87B Stuka, an advanced version of the aircraft. The 1:32 scale model features a sliding canopy, finely detailed cockpit, movable wheels and propeller, and two crew figures in flight outfits. The engine has a removable cowl.

F-15 Eagle. Among the key supersonic fighter planes of the 1970s is the F-15 Eagle, developed by McDonnell-Douglas for the U.S. Air Force and for sale to other countries. In 1973, the F-15 Eagle joined the fighter attack force of the Air Force Tactical Air Command. It is also used by Israel's air force. Extremely maneuverable, the single-seat fighter is designed for use as an interceptor-attack plane as well as for offensive assignments against ground forces. Powered by two huge 29,000-pound engines, it is capable of speeds in excess of 1200 miles per hour. The F-15 Eagle is heavily armed: it is generally equipped with advanced Sidewinder and Sparrow air-to-air missiles as well as internally mounted multibarrel machine guns (20mm or 25mm).

The plastic model shown here (16) is from Revell in 1:48 scale; but the F-15 Eagle is very popular with modelers today and is produced in different scales by many companies including Entex, Monogram, and Minicraft/Hasegawa.

B-29 Superfortress. The B-29 Superfortress bomber, one of the most famous planes in American aviation history, was developed in 1944 for one primary purpose—to attack the Japanese mainland in World War II. What the U.S. needed was a huge bomber that could carry large bomb loads to Japan from U.S. air bases in China, the Pacific islands and India. The largest bomber of its era, the Boeing B-29 was capable of carrying a bomb load of 18,000

14

15

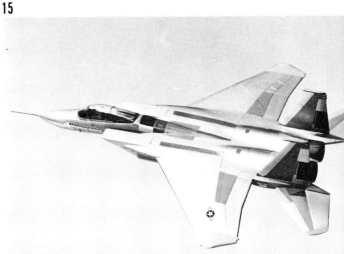

16

Aircraft from Revell: F-4E Phantom II (14), Junkers Stuka (15), and F-15 Eagle (16).

pounds and had a round-trip range of 4000 miles. All B-29s were concentrated under one command, the U.S. 20th Air Force, and by the end of the war there were approximately 1000 of them in service in the Pacific Theater of Operations. Among the famous missions flown by B-29s were the devastating attacks against Tokyo and the low-altitude incendiary bombings of Japanese industrial cities that were launched from Guam and Saipan. But the most famous B-29 of all was the Enola Gay, which dropped the atomic bomb on Hiroshima on August 6, 1945. Three days later, another B-29 delivered a second atomic bomb, this time to the city of Nagasaki. After the war, the B-29s were replaced by jet bombers that were larger, faster, and capable of carrying greater bomb loads.

This model from Monogram (17), made of plastic in a scale of 1:48, is almost 25 inches long and has a wingspan of just over 35 inches. Along with the exceptionally well-detailed parts of the airplane itself, the kit includes figures of five crew members.

Focke-Wulf 190. Many military historians hold that the Focke-Wulf 190 was the finest fighter plane produced in Germany during World War II. It was fast, maneuverable, and heavily armed. The single-seat, piston-engine fighter also was the first aircraft to use a cockpit canopy that could be jettisoned. As good as it may have been, however, after 1940 it proved to be no match for the British Spitfires and the United States fighter planes that were on their way: the P-38s, P-47s and P-51s. Focke-Wulf 190 fighters were used on both western and eastern fronts during the war and played a role in the Battle of Britain. But like the other makes of planes in the *Luftwaffe,* they had all but dis-

appeared from the skies by 1945. The manufacturer of the German 190s also gave its name to the Focke-Wulf Aghelis, which is regarded by many as the world's first successful helicopter.

This model of the Focke-Wulf 190 (18) is from Monogram, molded in plastic at 1:48 scale.

Bell Huey Cobra. Vietnam was a helicopter war. These machines were ideally suited to guerrilla warfare: they were capable of ferrying troops to areas that were otherwise impossible to get to, and could provide air and artillery cover to troops in jungle skirmishes. The Bell Huey Cobra AH-1 was developed specifically to serve as an armed helicopter in Vietnam. The U.S. Army took possession of the first prototypes, and the marines later added them to their ranks, calling them Sea Cobras. The helicopter is capable of speeds of more than 200 miles per hour and has a maximum range of about 360 miles. The rotor is 44 feet in diameter. In the way of armament, the Bell Huey Cobra carries a turret-mounted, three-barrel 20mm cannon in its nose, and exterior attachments of miniguns, grenade launchers and/or rockets. The aircraft was designed so its arms capabilities could be easily adapted for different situations, and individual copters often had their own personalized armaments, specialized for the zone in which they were fighting.

This model (19), in plastic from Monogram, is a 1:72 scale version of the army's Huey Cobra and comes with one crew member.

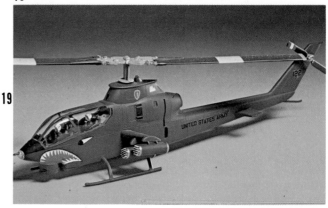

Model aircraft from Monogram: B-29 Superfortress (17), Germany's Focke-Wulf 190 (18), and the Bell Huey Cobra helicopter that saw action in Vietnam (19).

Displays and Dioramas

1 *Dioramas such as those created by Dave Elliott are beautiful examples of the modeler's art. This is the Sherman M4 A3.*

ALL MODELERS want to display their artistry and handiwork, and all collectors want to show off the handsome and unique items they've acquired. Good display is as much a part of military modeling as the researching, building, painting and detailing of the model.

Effective display is a craft that can involve a great deal of imagination, especially if you want to create a diorama, and often a good deal of carpentry skills if you plan to fashion stands, display cabinets, shadow boxes and the like. You can also buy many of these display items ready-made at a hobby shop, art supply store, lumberyard or department store.

A number of things must be taken into consideration before displaying military models. The military modeler deals with a number of different elements, just as the model railroader does, to create a plausible environment. For that reason, it is important to plan your display at the time you plan your

model building. If the finished product is to be mounted on a stand, for instance, it will help to decide what the stand will be made of, how big your display will be, how it will be decorated and where you will locate it. You will find your work will be easier and less frustrating if you work out these details at the very outset.

Many of the models shown in this book are mounted on stands of wood or plastic. This method enhances the appearance of the model and provides a convenient means of handling it. If you pick up the model itself, you run the risk of damaging it. Glass or clear plastic covers can also be bought or made to keep dirt and dust off the model.

Bookshelves are a popular display area for military models. If you plan to build a display shelf system yourself, the shelves can be built so they slant forward to give a better view of the model. Tacks or small blocks of wood can be used to hold the model in place on the shelf.

An important thing to remember is that you should not display your models in direct sunlight or in any other hot area such as near a radiator or heat register, because heat can warp a plastic model and damage paint. Be sure that if you add electric lighting to your cabinet or shadow box, or simply concentrate a light on your display, it does not radiate too much heat.

Many military modelers today integrate their displays by displaying figures with tanks, or aircraft and jeeps together, for instance. A complete trench warfare scene from World War I incorporating doughboys in the trench, artillery backing them up, and an old turret tank can be an interesting and handsome display.

Such a combination of elements into a single, three-dimensional scene is called a diorama. A diorama can be a permanent scene on its own base or can be a simpler grouping of individual elements. Dioramas have become so popular recently

that today you can purchase whole diorama kits. Many well-known model manufacturers, like Monogram, MRC-Tamiya, and US Airfix, offer full diorama kits with all parts included and detailed instructions on how to construct the entire scene.

The ultimate in diorama building, however, comes as an individual creation of the modeler. It is an area where a modeler can convert existing figures; customize other models through weathering, for example, or intentionally damage a tank or plane to make it look disabled; and add numerous details such as stretchers, sandbags and shrubbery that are made from scratch. You will have to plan this kind of diorama as an architect plans a building, or as a general plans a battle.

What you can do in this area of modeling is shown on the pages that follow. This sampling of various dioramas includes some that are made from kits, and others that were designed and built entirely by imaginative military modelers who used components from a variety of sources.

2

3

Dioramas take many forms. In some cases, modelers restrict the diorama to a single vehicle, such as Terry Gawriluk did when he created the German half-track display (2). Other modelers combine parts of several kits and fashion other components from scratch to create their miniature scenes, like John Wager did in his construction of the French antitank diorama (3). It's all a matter of the builder's taste and talents.

French Antitank Gun & Soldiers. Fighting the German tank in World War II was indeed a crucial and difficult task, as the British learned in the deserts of North Africa and the French experienced on their own soil. This diorama (3) depicts one of those moments as the French made a last-ditch effort in 1940 to hold off the advancing tanks and infantry of the German forces who were overrunning their land. But their small artillery, sandbag emplacements, and inexperienced and poorly trained troops were no match for the powerful German armies. This diorama, done to an approximate 1:35 scale and using 54mm figures, utilizes plastic figures and a plastic model of a 25mm antitank gun from Polk/Heller. The rest of the material, including the sandbags, were scratch-built.

George Rogers Clark Attacks Ft. Sackville. One way to dramatically display a diorama is a lighted shadow box. In this combination of kit figures and scratch-built items (4), George Rogers Clark is de-

picted leading an attack on Fort Sackville in 1778. The battle was only one of many into which Clark led his militia against British troops and Indians in Ohio, Illinois and Indiana during the American Revolution. Clark's force of volunteer militiamen numbered only about 175, but it was able to capture two important forts—Kaskaskia in Illinois and Vincennes in Indiana—in the same year that it took Fort Sackville.

Clark's expedition into the frontier states enabled the Americans to gain and hold control over that area, which proved to be important as the War of Independence progressed and after the war when the territory was awarded to the U.S. because of its domination there.

This diorama is made of converted figures from Imrie/Risley and a defunct Canadian firm, Jackson. The lifelike "trees" are roots, treated and finished realistically; the "water" was fashioned from plastic casting resin. The lighted shadow box highlights the scene and provides good protection.

4 *Roy Andersen's diorama of George Rogers Clark is built into a lighted display case.*

5 *Modeler Ron Hillman has created an extremely realistic scene of the Scot's Greys and French at Waterloo.*

Charge of the Scot's Greys. The Battle of Waterloo in 1815 is perhaps the single most "dioramatized" combat in military modeling, possibly because there are so many colorful, dramatic, and historically significant scenes that can be re-created from that battle. In this scene (5), a group of French infantrymen are under assault from a charge of the Scot's Greys who are followed into battle by a troop of Gordon Highlanders. These Gordon Highlanders were called "hangers-on" because, as shown here, they hung on to the tails of the horses that they followed. This diorama, in 30mm scale, was built a number of years ago using metal models from the British firm of Suren. Most were converted to adapt to the scene; the base and other decoration were scratch-built.

Sherman Mark 2C Firefly. The Sherman Mark 2C Firefly, like the one modeled in this diorama (6,7,8), was an American-made tank that was exported to Britain during World War II. The British added their own 17-pounder cannons to the tanks and used them extensively in France and Germany after the D-Day invasion in June 1944.

The diorama depicts the Mark 2 Firefly with British figures in a scene of rubble and destruction that was a common sight on the European continent in the last year of the war. The Mark 2C Firefly is a converted model from a Monogram plastic kit in 1:32 scale. The tank was converted by the addition of applique armor to the sides and the scratch-building of a new suspension system, gun hatch, and turret. Also added were a radio box at the rear

6

8

Expert detailing is evident in three views of modeler Dave Elliott's Sherman Mark 2C diorama (6,7,8).

7

of the turret and a muzzle break at the tip of the tank's cannon.

Other spare parts were also added for the sake of realism:the first-aid kit, and the tarps on the rear of the vehicle, made of rolled-up facial tissue with glue brushed on as a fixative; British personnel were customized from plastic figures made by US Airfix in 54mm scale; the shell of the bombed-out building was scratch-built from 1/4-inch fiberboard; and the ground cover is crushed flagstone.

Japanese Banzai Charge. The battles for the islands in the Pacific were savage and bloody. The names have become famous—Iwo Jima, Tarawa, Guadalcanal, Saipan and Okinawa. Japan fought back with desperation through the Gilbert Islands, the Solomons, the Marshall Islands, the Marianas, and finally the Philippines. Much of the fighting was in the jungles and rain forests and it was often hand-to-hand, with bayonets and with rifles used as clubs. "Banzai" was the cry the Japanese used as they rushed from their jungle cover to the attack.

Each island that had been occupied by the Japanese eventually fell, however, to the U.S. Marines and the U.S. Army infantrymen. Some banzai charges were suicidal missions, such as the Japanese kamikaze airplane attacks. Surrender was not a part of the Japanese military method. Most soldiers chose to die or hide out in caves—perhaps to starve to death—rather than give up to the American forces.

This diorama (9) memorializes one of the banzai charges on one of the islands somewhere in the Pacific in World War II. All the figures are from US Airfix, made of plastic in 1:32 scale. The scene is mounted on a separate wood base with scratch-built terrain.

M-16 Half-Track. The U.S. Army made many uses of the versatile, armored half-track during World War II. The one featured in this diorama (10), an M-16, was adapted and outfitted as a self-propelled piece of anti-aircraft artillery. The surrounding scene could be any town in France or Belgium in the last year of the war.

The M-16 model here was built without modification, directly from the kit and instructions provided by MRC-Tamiya. It is plastic, in a 1:35 scale. The American soldiers are converted figures from MRC-Tamiya, and the streetlight is from an MRC accessory kit.

The rest of the diorama was scratch-built. The building is fashioned from 1/4-inch Masonite, and the ground cover is crushed flagstone glued to the diorama base. The sidewalk, only a portion of which is visible in front of the building, is Masonite covered with spackle. The base was handmade from 3/4-inch plywood and was covered with walnut veneer.

Winter in the Ardennes. This winter diorama (11) depicts a cold, quiet scene at a United States field hospital somewhere in the Ardennes Forest of Belgium during the brutal winter of 1944. After the D-Day invasion, troops from the United States, Britain and Canada moved across France and Belgium, chipping away at the vast territory that had been held by the Germans. In the winter, the Germans opened their last counteroffensive, a strong but futile attack in the area of the Ardennes. Famous battles like Bastogne and the Battle of the Bulge were fought in the snow and freezing temperatures of winter. Thousands of casualties were treated in the makeshift tents of the field hospitals in these desolate areas; from there the wounded would be sent back to military hospitals away from the front lines.

The diorama has been built in a 1:35 scale, with basic model kits, some conversion, and some

9

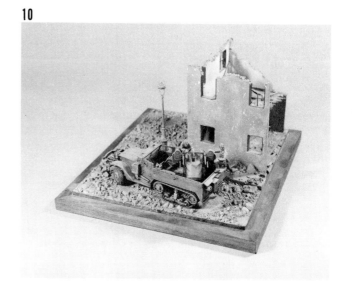

10

Dioramas can be made up of figures, like Paul Polloway's Banzai Charge scene (9), or vehicles, like Dave Elliott's halftrack (10).

11

12

13

The winter scene with Red Cross truck (11) is the work of Jim St. Louis; the tank assault diorama (12, 13) was created by Dave Elliott.

scratch-building. The vehicle, a U.S. Army 3/4-ton Dodge ambulance, is from a kit produced by Peerless. It has been given full interior detail. The figures are conversions of MRC-Tamiya models, and the tent and trees were built from scratch. The snow was made from ordinary baking soda.

Sherman M4 A3. The Sherman M4 was the most famous American tank to fight on the battlefields of World War II, and it was manufactured so that it could be adapted for various uses. The Sherman tank in this diorama (12,13) is the M4 A3, a specialized version that was used by the U.S. Army mainly

14 *MRC-Tamiya makes all the pieces shown in this "German Artillery Attack" scene. Once the figures and weaponry have been painted carefully, the modeler can construct a base that adds to the display's realism.*

in the sweep across Europe during late 1944 and early 1945.

The model here is a striking example of what can be done with model conversion. The basic Sherman M4 plastic kit from Monogram in 1:32 scale was used, and converted to resemble an M4 A3. The entire rear deck was removed and an M4 A3 deck was scratch-built. Louvered panels for the engine hatches were added; the rear hull was built up; the exhaust system was modified; and the tank was given a new and appropriate suspension system. Applique armor was added to the sides of the vehicle and to the turret and front hatches. A Cullin hedge-row device at the bow of the tank, which was used to shear hedges apart so they would not get caught up or tangled in the tracks of the tank, came with the Monogram model. The figures were converted from a model provided by MRC-Tamiya. The bushes were scratch-built from real twigs and roots and covered with foam rubber; the colors are the result of airbrushing eight different shades of green modeler's paint. The ground cover was also airbrushed.

German Artillery Attack. In the entire history of warfare, no country had unleashed attacks with such ferocity as did Germany with its blitzkrieg sieges against France, Belgium and Poland during the early days of World War II. The German Army was exceptionally well-equipped; its soldiers were highly trained. Battles were planned in detail and the coordination between infantry, artillery and armor was extraordinarily impressive. By the end of 1940, most of Europe had fallen to the advancing German forces; then Hitler's troops dug in. The same artillery and armor that had been used to conquer the land was then used as a stationary defense. But it was not enough to drive back the combined force of the United States, England, Canada, and the underground forces of France and Belgium.

This diorama (14) shows a typical artillery scene, complemented with some armor equipment, that could depict an offensive maneuver as well as a defensive stand, and could represent *Wehrmacht* soldiers in a setting anywhere between 1939 and 1945. The diorama uses MRC-Tamiya figures and vehicles exclusively. The artillery is an 88mm gun originally designed as an anti-aircraft gun but also used later in the war as an antitank weapon. In the background is a German 8-ton semitrack armored personnel carrier. The figures and equipment are all plastic, in a scale of 1:35.

Sources

Associations and Organizations

International Plastic Modelers Society/USA
P.O. Box 2555
Long Beach, CA 90801

Military modelers will be interested in the modeling activities covered by IPMS/USA. All kinds of modeling in plastics are the organization's interest—military vehicles, figures, ships and airplanes. It is the largest organization in the United States for static model builders, currently serving about 5000 active members. Chapters are located in various parts of the country. IPMS/USA issues two publications to its members: *Update* and *IPMS/USA Quarterly.*

The organization also sponsors competitions, and provides guidelines and rules for them so you can organize your own on a local level. A national convention is held each year. Dues are $10 a year for adults and $6 for those under 18 years of age. Membership includes free subscriptions to both IPMS/USA magazines.

Periodicals

MAGAZINES offer a specific package of benefits to the modeler. News of current events in the hobby, articles of specific interest, tips, idea exchanges, and new product reviews are just some of the things the modeler can find in these publications. The following are the major magazines of interest to the military modeler.

Air Classics, Challenge Publications, Inc., 7950 Deering Ave., Canoga Park, CA 91304. Although this magazine does contain photographs and stories about nonmilitary aircraft, its emphasis is on planes that saw combat. Like *Air Combat,* also published by Challenge, *Air Classics* can be very helpful to modelers who want their replicas to look as much like the real thing as possible. This monthly magazine is available on newsstands, at hobby shops and by subscription.

Air Combat, Challenge Publications, Inc., 7950 Deering Ave., Canoga Park, CA 91304. Composed almost entirely of photographs and articles about real combat planes, this bimonthly magazine can be of great value to modelers who strive for authen-

ticity in decorating their military aircraft replicas. Available on newsstands, at hobby shops and by subscription.

Airfix Magazine for Modelers, Surridge Dawson and Company Ltd., Publishing Dept., 136/142 New Kent Road, London SE1, England. Although it carries the name of a large model manufacturing company, *Airfix Magazine* contains news of many other brands of models, and contains historical photographs to aid the modeler in decorating them realistically. Drawings, news of books and other products, and want ads from around the world are also included. Available on some newsstands, at hobby shops and by subscription.

International Modeler, Sensory Perceptions, P.O. Box 1208, Topanga, CA 90290. Subtitled "Model Building for the Adult Modeler," this relatively new publication offers well-illustrated articles on various forms of static modeling. Military models are covered, but perhaps not as frequently as are car models. A good classified ad section lists opportunities to buy or swap modeling equipment and tools as well as collectibles. *International Modeler* is published bimonthly and is available by subscription or at some newsstands and hobby shops.

IPMS/USA Quarterly, International Plastic Modelers Society/USA, P.O. Box 2555, Long Beach, CA 90801. This is the classier of the two IPMS/USA official publications: each issue has more pages and is broader in scope than its companion publication *Update*. The *Quarterly* usually contains an excellent collection of in-depth articles on many areas of static plastic modeling, written by those who are really experts in the hobby. Military models (including figures) are covered well, and airplane modeling is generally the subject of special emphasis. The magazine is published four times a year; it comes automatically with membership in the IPMS/USA.

Military Modeler, Challenge Publications Inc., 7950 Deering Ave., Canoga Park, CA 91304. This is a magazine thoroughly devoted to military modeling. Articles with titles like "Napoleon's Generals," "Weapons of the Wehrmacht," and "The Yom Kippur M48 Tank" will give you an idea of the magazine's audience. Regular features are "Pass in Review," a look at what's new in military miniature figures; and "Armor in Review," which catalogs new releases of various kinds of military models. The ideas and experiences of master modelers add up to a well-rounded and highly interesting publication for the military modeler. Tips, "how-to" articles, product and book reviews, and effective illustrations are all included. *Military Modeler* is published monthly. It is available by subscription, and at many newsstands and hobby shops.

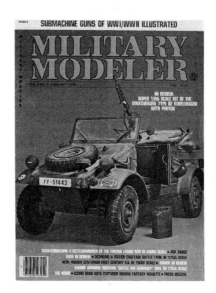

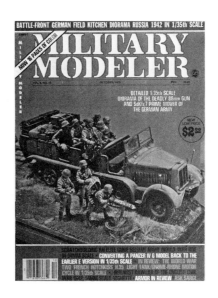

Scale Aircraft Modeler, Challenge Publications Inc., 7950 Deering Ave., Canoga Park, CA 91304. The military modeler who specializes in aircraft will be interested in this publication. All aspects of building and decorating static model airplanes are offered in this quarterly publication. It contains solid articles from accomplished airplane modelers and good illustrations. Available by subscription, and at some newsstands and hobby shops.

Scale Modeler, Challenge Publications Inc., 7950 Deering Ave., Canoga Park, CA 91304. This is one of the most popular magazines in the hobby world. It covers every form of static modeling, from cars to planes to military items. Good articles, sharp product reviews, and plenty of ideas and tips are included in each monthly issue. It calls itself the "world's largest modeling magazine," a statement that refers to its readership. It can be found on most newsstands and in most hobby shops.

Scale Models, Model & Allied Publications Ltd., P.O. Box 35, Bridge Street, Hemel Hempstead, Herts HP1 1EE, England. Published by the British firm that also publishes *Military Modelling, Scale Models* is directed more toward modelers of military vehicles than to modelers of figures. Issues contain diagrams, full-color drawings, illustrated step-by-step assembly tips, features on modelers and many advertisements. Available on newsstands, at hobby shops and by subscription.

Military Modelling, Model & Allied Publications Ltd., P.O. Box 35, Bridge Street, Hemel Hempstead, Herts, HP1 1EE, England. This British publication is filled with beautiful photography of dioramas, drawings, resource material, news of products, and advertisements from United States and foreign manufacturers. Much of the magazine is devoted to military figures. Copies are available on newsstands or by subscription (send self-addressed, stamped envelope to publisher for further information).

Update, International Plastic Modelers Society/ USA, P.O. Box 2555, Long Beach, CA 90801. This is the official newsletter of IPMS/USA and the periodical that keeps all members on top of what is going on in the hobby as well as in the organization. Good articles are always included, as are a lot of tips, techniques, and innovations. Its coverage of competitions, chapter meetings and other organization events are of interest to most modelers. *Update* is published every other month. Subscription is included with membership in IPMS/USA.

Manufacturers and Distributors

DISTRIBUTORS AND manufacturers of modeling products provide a number of valuable services to the hobbyist. Most of the companies listed below publish catalogs, many of which are very beautifully illustrated and informative. These can give you an idea of what is available and how much you can expect to pay for it. Many of these firms also publish how-to booklets and other materials that provide helpful hints about the use of their products.

ARMOR AND ARTILLERY

Bandai (See Polk's)

ESCI (See Scale Craft)

GHQ Wargame Miniatures
2634 Bryant Ave., South
Minneapolis, MN 55408

Heller (See Polk's)

H-R Products
P.O. Box 67
McHenry, IL 60050

Italaeri (See Revell)

Life-Like Products Inc.
1600 Union Ave.
Baltimore, MD 21211

Minicraft/Hasegawa
1510 W. 228th St.
Torrance, CA 90501

Mitsuwa (See Scale Craft)

Monogram Models
8601 Waukegan Rd.
Morton Grove, IL 60053

MRC-Tamiya
2500 Woodbridge Ave.
Edison, NJ 08817

Nitto Kagaku (See Scale Craft)

Otaki (See Scale Craft)

Peerless Corp.
3919 M St.
Philadelphia, PA 19124

Polk/Heller (See Polk's)

Polk's Model Craft Hobbies
314 Fifth Ave.
New York, NY 10001

Revell Inc.
4223 Glencoe Ave.
Venice, CA 90291

Scale Craft Models Inc.
8735 Shirley Ave.
Northridge, CA 91324

Solido
Euro Imports
19H Gardner Rd.
Fairfield, NJ 07006

Tamiya (See MRC-Tamiya)

MILITARY AIRCRAFT

Airtec
128 South Rd.
Enfield, CT 06082

AMT
Lesney AMT Corp.
3031 James St.
Baltimore, MD 21230

Aristo-Craft Models (See Polk's)

Bachmann Bros. Inc.
1400 Erie Ave.
Philadelphia, PA 19124

Entex Industries
1100 W. Walnut St.
Compton, CA 90220

ESCI (See Scale Craft)

Fujimi
Calex
1510 W. 228th St.
Torrance, CA 90501

Heller (See Polk's)

J & L Aircraft Models
P.O. Box 6004
Torrance, CA 90504

Krasel Industries Inc.
1821 E. Newport Circle
Santa Ana, CA 92705

Lindberg Products Inc.
8050 N. Monticello Ave.
Skokie, IL 60076

LS Models (See Scale Craft)

Military Model Distributors
1115 Crowley Dr.
Carrollton, TX 75006

Minicraft/Hasegawa
1510 W. 228th St.
Torrance, CA 90501

Monogram Models
8601 Waukegan Rd.
Morton Grove, IL 60053

MPC
General Mills Fun Group Inc.
Mount Clemens, MI 48045

MRC-Tamiya
2500 Woodbridge Ave.
Edison, NJ 08817

Otaki (See Scale Craft)

Polk/Heller (See Polk's)

Polk's Model Craft Hobbies
346 Bergen Ave.
Jersey City, NJ 07304

Revell Inc.
4223 Glencoe Ave.
Venice, CA 90291

Scale Craft Models Inc.
8735 Shirley Ave.
Northridge, CA 91324

Tamiya (See MRC-Tamiya)

US Airfix
AVA International
P.O. Box 7611
Waco, TX 76710

MILITARY SHIPS

Alnavco
P.O. Box 9
Belle Haven, VA 23306

Aristo-Craft Models (See Polk's)

Heller (See Polk's)

Heritage Models Inc.
9840 Monroe Drive, Building 106
Dallas, TX 75220

Imai (See Scale Craft)

Life-Like Products Inc.
1600 Union Ave.
Baltimore, MD 21211

Lindberg Products Inc.
8050 N. Monticello Ave.
Skokie, IL 60076
Mantua Metal Products
Grandview Ave.
Woodbury Heights, NJ 08097
Minicraft/Hasegawa
1510 W. 228th St.
Torrance, CA 90501
Monogram Models
8601 Waukegan Rd.
Morton Grove, IL 60053
MRC-Tamiya
2500 Woodbridge Ave.
Edison, NJ 08817
Nichimo (See Coulter-Bennett)
Otaki (See Scale Craft)
Polk/Heller (See Polk's)
Polk's Model Craft Hobbies
346 Bergen Ave.
Jersey City, NJ 07304
Revell Inc.
4223 Glencoe Ave.
Venice, CA 90291
Scale Craft Models Inc.
8735 Shirley Ave.
Northridge, CA 91324
Scientific Models Inc.
340 Snyder Ave.
Berkeley Heights, NJ 07922
Sterling Models Inc.
Belfield Avenue & Wister St.
Philadelphia, PA 19144
Tamiya (See MRC-Tamiya)
US Airfix
AVA International
P.O. Box 7611
Waco, TX 76710
Valiant Miniatures
P.O. Box 394
Skokie, IL 60076

MILITARY FIGURES

Alnavco
P.O. Box 8
Belle Haven, VA 23306
Alymer (See Polk's)
Aristo-Craft Models (See Polk's)
Associated Hobby Manufacturers
401 E. Tioga St.
Philadelphia, PA 19134
Atlantic North America Inc.
3100 Bayside Drive
Palatine, IL 60067
Bivouac Military Miniatures
P.O. Box 12522
Kansas City, MO 64116
Black Watch
P.O. Box 666
Van Nuys, CA 91408

Boyd Models
1835 Whittier Ave.
Building B-1
Costa Mesa, CA 92627
Britains Ltd.
Walthamstow
London E-17, England
Cameo Personalities
P.O. Box 3035
Glendale, CA 91201
Cavalier Miniatures
105 Jamaica Ave.
Brooklyn, NY 11027
Charles Miniatures (See Coulter-Bennett)
> **Coulter-Bennett Ltd.**
12158 Hamlin St.
North Hollywood, CA 91606
CS & D
731 S. University Blvd.
Denver, CO 80209
Dave Casciano Co.
314 Edgley Ave.
Glenside, PA 19038
Garrison Miniatures (See Coulter-Bennett)
Greenwood & Ball Ltd. (See Coulter-Bennett)
Grenadier Miniatures
118 Lynbrooke Rd.
Springfield, PA 19063
Heritage Models Inc.
9840 Monroe Drive
Building 106
Dallax, TX 75220
Hinchcliffe Models (See Heritage Models)
Historex (See Coulter-Bennett)
History in Metal
P.O. Box 451
Chagrin Falls, OH 44022
Imrie/Risley Miniatures Inc.
P.O. Box 89
Burnt Hills, NY 12027
Jack Scruby's Miniatures
P.O. Box 1658
Cambria, CA 93428
Jose Almirall (See Polk's)
K and L Co.
P.O. Box 3781
Tulsa, OK 74152
Lasset Miniatures (See Coulter-Bennett)
Little Generals
P.O. Box 8646
Kansas City, MO 64114
Lou Zocchi & Associates
7604 Newton Drive
Biloxi, MS 39532
Merite (See Polk's)
Miniature Figurines Ltd.
P.O. Box P
Pine Plains, NY 12567

Minimen
P.O. Box 451
Chagrin Falls, OH 44022

Monarch
P.O. Box 4195
Long Island City, NY 11104

MRC-Tamiya
2500 Woodbridge Ave.
Edison, NJ 08817

Old Guard Inc.
33 N. Main St.
New Hope, PA 18938

Phoenix Miniatures (See Coulter-Bennett)

Polk/Heller (See Polk's)

→**Polk's Model Craft Hobbies**
346 Bergen Ave.
Jersey City, NJ 07304

Poste Militaire (See Coulter-Bennett)

Reeves International
1107 Broadway
New York, NY 10010

Ronald Wall Figurines Ltd.
7370 Pasadena Ave.
St. Louis, MO 63121

Sanderson (See Coulter-Bennett)

Segom
Model Figures and Hobbies
Lower Balloo Road
Groomsport, N. Ireland

Series 77 Miniatures
P.O. Box 1141
Canoga Park, CA 91304

Sovereign Miniatures (See Coulter-Bennett)

Squadron/Rubin Miniatures
3461 E. Ten Mile Rd.
Warren, MI 48091

Stadden (See Coulter-Bennett)

Superior Models (See Coulter-Bennett)

Tamiya (See MRC-Tamiya)

Tom Loback Artworks
150 W. 26th St.
New York, NY 10001

US Airfix
AVA International
P.O. Box 7611
Waco, TX 76710

←**Valiant Miniatures**
P.O. Box 394
Skokie, IL 60076

WRW Imports Inc.
3730 Wheeling St.
Denver, CO 80239

ASSEMBLY MATERIALS AND TOOLS

Armtec
128 South R.
Enfield, CT 06082

Baca Products
19 Hawthorne Lane
Streamwood, IL 60103

Badger Air-Brush Co.
9128 W. Belmont Ave.
Franklin Park, IL 60131

Balsa USA
P.O. Box 164
Marinette, WI 54143

Bammco
P.O. Box 1334
Canoga Park, CA 91304

B & D Enterprises
P.O. Box 2268, Pike Station
Rockville, MD 20852

Brice Machine Specialties
14722 Leahy Ave.
Bellflower, CA 90706

BWT Systems
161 Anita Drive
Pickerington, OH 43147

Carmel Industries Inc.
50-20 25th St.
Long Island City, NY 11101

CPC
777 W. Grand Ave.
Oakland, CA 94612

Custom Craft Products
19 Florgate Rd.
Farmingdale, NY 11735

DA Enterprises
P.O. Box 335
Haubstadt, IN 47639

Delta Manufacturing
P.O. Box 27
Lorimor, IA 50149

Dixon Company
750 Washington Ave.
Carlstadt, NJ 07072

Dremel Manufacturing
4915 21st St.
Racine, WI 53406

Du Bro Products Inc.
480 Bonner Rd.
Wauconda, IL 60084

Duro Art Supply Co.
1832 Juneway Terrace
Chicago, IL 60626

EMG Engineering Co.
18518 S. Broadway
Gardena, CA 90248

F.A.I. Model Supply
1800 W. Hatcher Rd.
Phoenix, AZ 85021

Floquil
Route 30
North Amsterdam, NY 12010

Fox Manufacturing Co.
5305 Towson Ave.
Fort Smith, AR 72901

Grabber
P.O. Box 337
Hwy. 56 West
Edgerton, KS 60021

Griffin Manufacturing Co.
1656 Ridge Rd.
East Webster, NY 14580

Grumbacher Inc.
460 W. 34th St.
New York, NY 10001

Hobbypoxy
36 Pine St.
Rockaway, NJ 07866

Hobsco Inc.
P.O. Box 18133
Milwaukee, WI 53218

Humbrol Paints
(See Model Rectifier)

Jim Crocket
1442 N. Fruit Ave.
Fresno, CA 93728

K & B Manufacturing
12152 Woodruff Ave.
Downey, CA 90241

K & S Engineering
6917 W. 59th St.
Chicago, IL 60638

Kemtron Corp.
P.O. Box 360
Walnut, CA 91789

Kibri
100 Main St.
Reading, MA 01867

Krasel Industries, Inc.
1821 E. Newport Circle
Santa Ana, CA 92705

Microflame Inc.
3724 Oregon Ave. South
Minneapolis, MN 55426

The K. J. Miller Corp.
2401 Gardner Rd.
Broadview, IL 60153

Model Builder Products
621 W. 19th St.
Costa Mesa, CA 92627

Model Rectifier Corp.
2500 Woodbridge Ave.
Edison, NJ 08817

Paasche Air-Brush Co.
1909 W. Diversey Parkway
Chicago, IL 60614

Pactra Industries
7060 Hollywood Blvd.
Los Angeles, CA 90028

Panarise
10107 Adella Ave.
South Gate, CA 90803

Permanent Pigments
1100 Church Lane
Easton, PA 18042

Pettit Paint Co., Inc.
20 Pine St.
Rockway, NY 07866

Po Instrument Co.
13 Lehigh Ave.
Patterson, NJ 07503

Prather Products
1660 Ravenna Ave.
Wilmington, CA 96744

Precision Manufacturing Co.
4546 Sinclair Rd.
San Antonio, TX 78222

Progress Manufacturing Co.
P.O. Box 912
Manhattan, KS 66052

Royal Products Corp.
790 W. Tennessee St.
Denver, CO 80223

Scalecoat Quality Craft Models, Inc.
177 Wheatley Ave.
Northumberland, PA 17857

Sullivan Products Inc.
535 Davisville Rd.
Willow Grove, PA 19090

Su-Pr-Line Products
Plainfield, IL 60544

Tatone Products Corp.
1208 Geneva Ave.
San Francisco, CA 94112

Testor Corp.
620 Buckbee St.
Rockford, IL 61101

Thorp Manufacturing
1655 E. Mission Blvd.
Pomona, CA 91766

Top Flite
1901 N. Narragansett Ave.
Chicago, IL 60639

Twinn-K Inc.
10296 W. Washington St.
P.O. Box 31228
Indianapolis, IN 46231

V L Products
7023-D Canoga Ave.
Canoga Park, CA 91303

V.M.W. Co.
1640 E. Edinger Ave.
Santa Ana, CA 92705

Wen Products
5801 Northwest Hwy.
Chicago, IL 60631

Williams Bros.
181 Pawnee St.
San Marcos, CA 92069

Wing Manufacturing
P.O. Box 33
Crystal Lake, IL 60014

X-Acto Inc.
45-35 Van Dam St.
Long Island City, NY 11101

Zona Saws (See F.A.I. Model Supply)

Advice from the Experts

The hobby of assembling and decorating military models is as much an art as a craft.

Experienced modelers often meet to discuss the craftsmanship of putting their miniature replicas together and decorating them with great authenticity and detail.

All expert modelers encounter similar problems, but they develop different techniques to solve them. A wide variety of tips is available to modelers who keep their eyes open for ways to continually improve the looks of their models and dioramas. The ability to put these tips to use is what separates the true military artists from the casual hobbyists.

On the following pages, we illustrate a number of tips suggested by experienced military model enthusiasts.

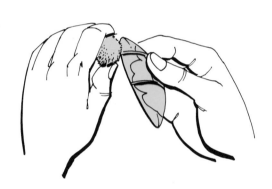

Clear plastic windshields and canopies should be washed with a solution of warm water and dishwashing liquid before you assemble the model. The washing will remove mold release and dust. Rinse in clear, warm water and blot with a cotton ball. Then store the part until it's needed to avoid scratches.

Masking should be done with masking tape. Good tapes will stretch slightly to conform to the contours of a model and won't lift paint off when peeled from the model's surface. Before applying paint over the masked area, seal the edges of the tape by applying pressure with the cap of a ball-point pen to prevent the paint from creeping underneath. Let the paint dry 15 minutes or less: longer drying times may result in chunks of paint lifting up with the tape.

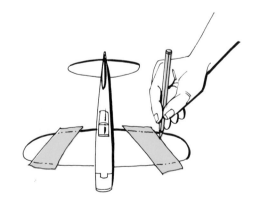

It's best to install canopies after painting the model. If this is impossible, however, you'll have to mask the clear plastic. Masking tape can be used for this, but it is much better to use a commercial masking liquid such as Micro Mask or Magic Masker. Brush it on and allow it to dry before painting. After painting, peel the masking material off the canopy.

To apply camouflage paint, spray a small amount of paint on a piece of waxed paper; mix with thinner and dab the paint onto the model with a piece of sponge.

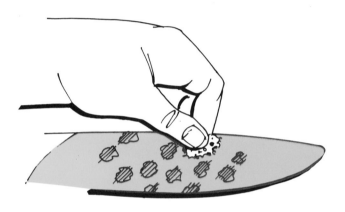

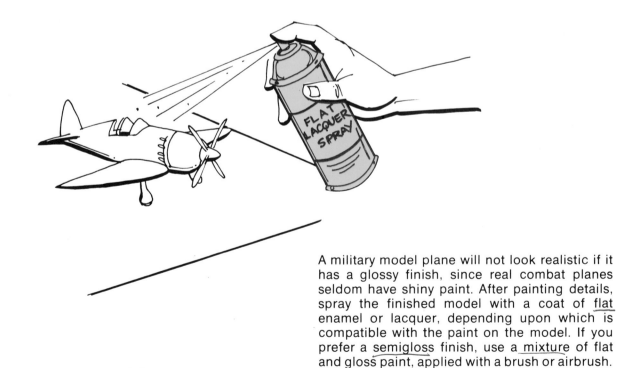

A military model plane will not look realistic if it has a glossy finish, since real combat planes seldom have shiny paint. After painting details, spray the finished model with a coat of <u>flat</u> enamel or lacquer, depending upon which is compatible with the paint on the model. If you prefer a <u>semigloss</u> finish, use a <u>mixture</u> of flat and gloss paint, applied with a brush or airbrush.

Weathering of a military plane model can be accomplished by several methods. An easy way is to coat the model with silver paint, mask the areas to be exposed by dabbing with liquid masking, and then give the model its final coat of paint. When you remove the masking, the silver paint will give the model a weathered appearance.

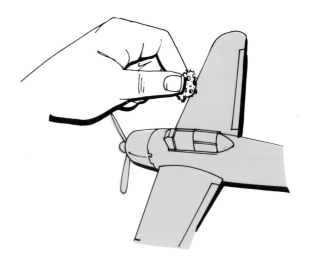

Engine oil leaks can be duplicated by using a black felt-tip pen. Draw a line from the point where the leak should begin, and then smear the ink with a damp cloth to run the leak pattern from the source. Spray the ink with clear paint to retain the effect.

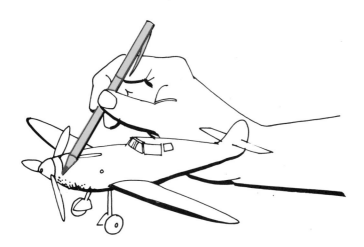

The weathering of military vehicle models is a three-part process. First, dry brush the entire model with a coat of yellowish brown paint to simulate dust and dirt; apply more paint to lower parts such as wheel wells, for realism using a scrubbing action to give a blotchy appearance to the finish. Next, add some white paint to the yellowish brown, and go over the model again, this time only hitting the highlights such as edges, rivets, seams and screws. Then add rust where appropriate by applying a base color of dark brown, then red, and finally bright orange to the parts that are to appear badly rusted.

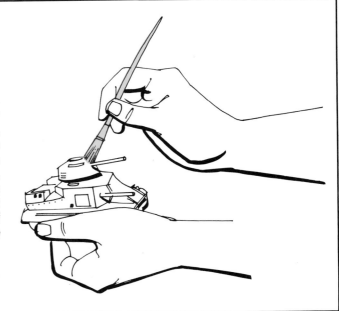

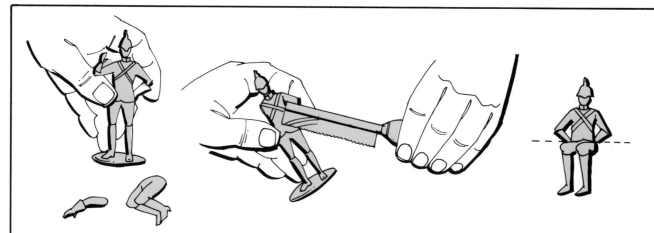

You can alter plastic or metal figures to adapt them to your particular diorama. It is possible to merely reposition body parts from a single figure, although it's sometimes necessary to take parts from several different figures to get the right effect. Cut the figures with a razor saw and reposition the arms, legs, head or other parts as you desire. Secure all parts with glue. The resulting gaps should then be filled with body putty (or solder for metal figures) and sanded.

To give fenders of military vehicle models a bent appearance, carefully heat the fender over a candle flame. Hold the part high over the flame to prevent melting, and test the malleability of the plastic periodically with a pencil eraser. When the plastic is soft enough, use the eraser to bend the fender to the desired shape. If the part looks melted rather than bent, use a hobby knife to scrape areas that have become rounded by the heat.

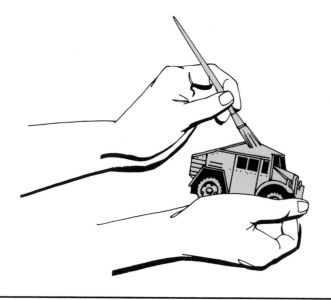

When weathering a model, use the technique known as dry brushing. Put only a small bit of paint on the brush and brush the surface of the model very lightly. You're doing it right if the paint only catches on the high points of the model's surface. A wide, flat red sable artist's brush is best for this type of painting.

Blanket and tent rolls can be made from facial tissue. Moisten the tissue, roll it and tie with thread. When dry, paint to the desired color and fasten to the model. You can make camouflage nets in much the same way using cheesecloth.

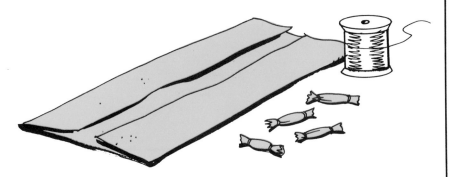

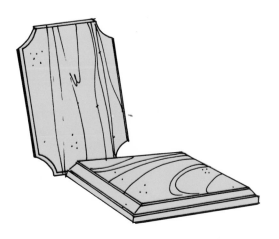

Decoupage plaques make excellent diorama bases, and are available from art supply stores. If you wish to build your own base, use plywood and allow a 3/4-inch border all the way around it. Don't forget to seal the base with shellac or varnish to prevent warping.

Paint faces of plastic and metal military figures with tan or light brown colors to simulate the suntanned skin color of a soldier. Also, remember that people in bright sunlight tend to squint. Paint the eyes so that they look like black slits; never paint whites in the eyes, because this will look the same color as the face at normal viewing distance. Shade the faces with flesh color, mixed with shades of red, brown and white. Make the differences in color dramatic, because subtle shading will not be noticed. Where you make drastic changes from light to dark color, blend the edge between the two colors using a brush moistened with turpentine.

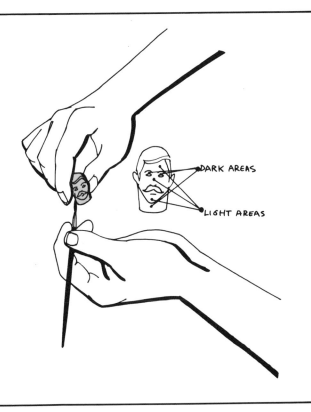

DARK AREAS

LIGHT AREAS

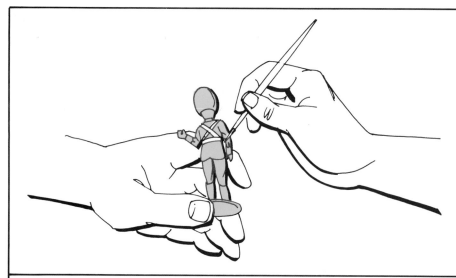

Represent the folds in clothing by shading with a darker color. Never make two articles of clothing the same shade. Vary the shades to represent different degrees of fading in the material.

You can dress up the edges of a plywood diorama base by gluing on strips of hardwood veneer. Finish with a coat of clear varnish.

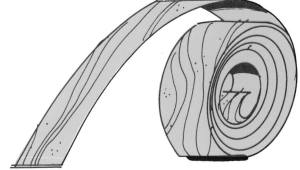

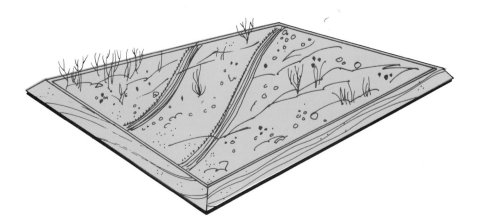

For the basic groundwork of your diorama, use slow-drying plaster or Celluclay, which is available from art supply stores. While the plaster is still wet, sprinkle it with pebbles and sand. Make tire tracks and footprints, and then use unravelled hemp rope or theatrical crepe hair to sim- ulate grass. Short grass can be depicted with sawdust. If you wish to color the plaster, dye it with food coloring while the plaster is wet. When the plaster is thoroughly dry, paint the ground yellowish green and the grass slightly brown for best results.

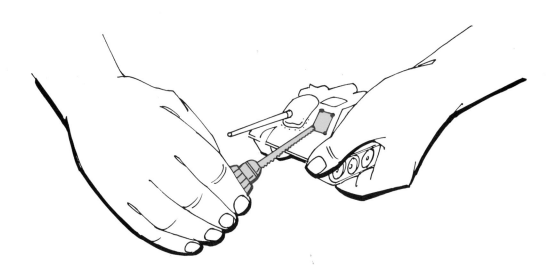

Open hatches in military vehicle models add to their realistic appearance. There are two ways to accomplish this. You can use two kits and cut the opening in the hull you'll use and cut the doors from the second hull. Or, you can save the cost of a second kit by using another procedure.

Drill a few closely spaced holes on the outside edge of the door, and then cut out the door with a razor saw. File or sand the edges of the opening. Since the opening is larger than the door at this point, glue strips of plastic to the edges of the opening to reduce its size.

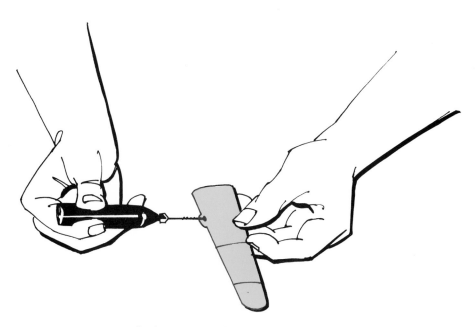

To give your military model a more realistic appearance, drill out the openings of gun barrels and exhaust pipes, using a modeler's drill. You can also cut slots and ports in tank hulls with a modeling saw or hobby knife.

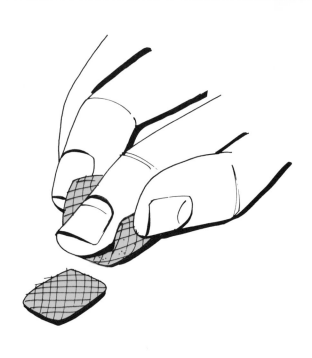

Sandbags can be made from epoxy putty or Play-doh. After shaping the bag, give it a burlap texture by wrapping a piece of a T-shirt over your finger and pressing the pattern into the putty. Finish off by adding rips and seams with a hobby knife.

Miniature barbed wire is easy to make. Drive two nails into a board, and stretch two strands of soft copper wire between them. Using the same type of wire, wrap the barbs onto the two strands at 3/8-inch intervals. Tie the barbs with long strands for easy handling. Then snip them to about 1/16 inch to finish.

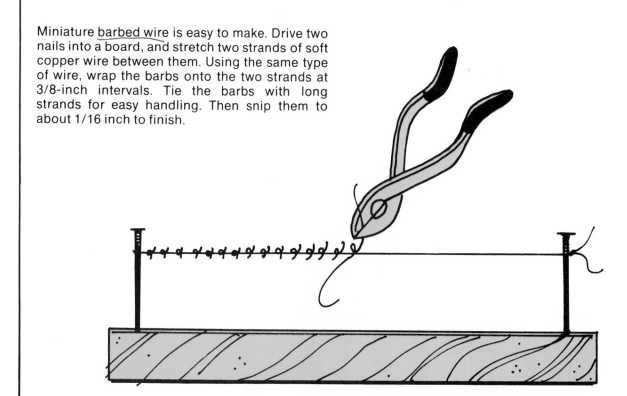